Dear Dad,

Happy Birthday!

always my dad, no matter how old we both become! Pxxx.

Ralph Mathekga

RAMAPHOSA'S
TURN

Can Cyril Save South Africa?

Tafelberg

Tafelberg
An imprint of NB Publishers, a Division of Media24 Boeke (Pty) Ltd
40 Heerengracht, Cape Town
www.tafelberg.com

Cover design: Mike Cruywagen
Book design: Nazli Jacobs
Editing: Russell Martin
Proofreading: Lisa Compton
Index: Sanet le Roux

First edition, first impression 2018

Printed by **novus print**, a Novus Holdings company

ISBN: 978-0-624-08554-6
Epub: 978-0-624-08555-3
Mobi: 978-0-624-08556-0

To my late grandmother Sophy,
for great childhood memories that still remain vivid

Contents

Foreword by Adriaan Basson

—∼∼—

The election of Matamela Cyril Ramaphosa as the ANC's thirteenth president in December 2017 represented a momentous turning point in the history of Africa's oldest liberation movement as well as of the country which it governs.

The misrule of Jacob Zuma, ably supported by his friends the Guptas and a slew of compromised keepers in key state institutions, brought the ANC within inches of extinction. Under Zuma, the party of Nelson Mandela, Oliver Tambo and Walter Sisulu became a vehicle for corrupt self-enrichment by a connected elite and compromised its founding values in a bid to shield the man from Nkandla and his detractors. Institutions were emasculated, government policy perverted, and civil servants corrupted to enrich Zuma and his cabal.

The scheme, now baptised "radical economic transformation"

(although Zuma himself did absolutely nothing to radically em-power black people during his term in office), was brought to an abrupt end at the concrete jungle in Nasrec when Ramaphosa defeated Nkosazana Dlamini-Zuma by the narrowest of margins in injury time. The shop-steward-turned-billionaire suddenly became the face of Operation Clean-up and gave millions of South Africans a reason to hope for the first time since Zuma took his oath of office in 2009.

As we at News24 tried to make sense of this historic moment, Ralph Mathekga was by our side to provide the necessary insight, logic and analysis in a moment of great political hype.

In an era of dial-a-quote commentators, Mathekga has distin-guished himself as one of South Africa's foremost thinkers and writers on government, power and politics. Never swayed by the prevailing hype, Mathekga swiftly brought us back to earth by reminding us and our readers that Ramaphosa was no messiah with a magic wand who would fix South Africa's many ills overnight. This superb book is a continuation of his analysis of Ramaphosa's stunning victory.

These were also trying times for the media. Under Zuma it be-came all too easy to accept and follow the clear-cut narrative of good versus bad. Zuma and his coterie of bandits were the baddies; those opposing him under Ramaphosa's banner were the good guys. But, as Mathekga has often reminded us, there ain't no easy answers.

In this book Mathekga outlines in a masterly way the challenges that Ramaphosa faces if he is to succeed. He takes us back to the new president's shaping years as an activist and trade unionist –

long before he became a public figure and earned his reputation as a skilled negotiator during the CODESA talks for a new South Africa.

The governing party emerged battered and bruised from the Nasrec conference and, despite the ANC's best attempts to make the country believe that it had emerged unified from this episode, the cracks were there for all to see.

Will Ramaphosa succeed in bringing together divergent interest groups under one common goal in his new role as president of the ANC and of South Africa?

Following his narrow victory at Nasrec, Ramaphosa opted for an aggressive approach. Even though only two of the candidates on his slate – Gwede Mantashe and Paul Mashatile – were elected with him as part of the ANC's "top six", Ramaphosa moved swiftly to eject Zuma from the Union Buildings. This was a calculated risk: Ramaphosa needed to make a symbolic statement to show the country he was in charge, but he couldn't effect wholesale changes and he was still left with a large chunk of Zuma administration members, who were now running affairs in his name.

In his book Mathekga grapples with important questions: Did Ramaphosa move too fast? Should he not have used the year and a bit before the 2019 national and provincial elections to solidify his power inside the ANC before making deep cuts to undo Zuma's state capture legacy?

The state-owned enterprises are a case in point. Ramaphosa moved in like an angry buffalo and removed the boards and executives of Eskom, Transnet and Denel in his first hundred days as president. These institutions were at the heart of Zuma's state capture project, and it will take much longer than a year and a bit to root out the corruption and mould them into functioning entities.

Ramaphosa will furthermore need the criminal justice system to be effective in dealing with the corrupt legacy of state capture. There is no use saying the right things and making the right moves politically, but nobody goes to jail.

There are signs that the Hawks and the National Prosecuting Authority have rediscovered their collective backbone after Ramaphosa's swearing-in, but the proof lies in the prosecution and imprisonment of the state capturers. This presents another quagmire for Ramaphosa: what is the political cost of going after senior ANC members before an election?

Mathekga interrogates this and other crucial questions. Can Ramaphosa clean up the ANC and South Africa, and win an election at the same time? Will he have to make some compromises along the way to ensure he consolidates his political power before "doing the right thing"?

It is no secret that many of Ramaphosa's comrades in the ANC were implicated, directly or indirectly, in the state capture project under Zuma. In his first cabinet reshuffle, Ramaphosa fired ten of those ministers deeply implicated in wrongdoing during Zuma's tenure.

But the fightback has begun and Ramaphosa faces serious opposition from KwaZulu-Natal, and from Mpumalanga, North West and the Free State – the three provinces that formed the backbone of the so-called Premier League, which was hoodwinked at the last minute by Mpumalanga's David Mabuza to prevent Dlamini-Zuma from taking over the ANC presidency. Can Ramaphosa risk losing the support of these provinces if he cuts too deep before the 2019 elections?

Mathekga's insightful analysis of Ramaphosa's many challenges naturally poses the question: why on earth would he want the job?

He earned his stripes in the fight against apartheid; he was a champion of workers' rights; he was an early pioneer of BEE, which created millionaires out of black entrepreneurs; and he always remained a senior member of the ANC. Was the position of ANC president, for which he was overlooked in favour of Thabo Mbeki after Nelson Mandela stepped down in 1999, the one accolade Ramaphosa always wanted and then finally achieved with the narrowest of margins in December 2017?

Ramaphosa's election may have saved the ANC from electoral defeat, but the jury is out on whether he can unify the majority of the party behind his vision for both the organisation and South Africa.

Mathekga's book is an excellent guide to understanding the road ahead for a leader whose time has at last come.

ADRIAAN BASSON
Cape Town, May 2018

Introduction

With the country trying to find its way again after a decade of rampant corruption in which state institutions were nearly decimated, many South Africans agree on one thing. Electing a billionaire as leader has at least one advantage: he is unlikely to steal from the people.

But why should a billionaire businessman want to be the president of a volatile society with such deep inequalities as ours? Clearly, it's a suicide mission. Maybe it has to do with an inflated male ego. If you doubt this explanation, just look at the picnic under way at the White House in the United States. If being a president merely provides personal fulfilment or satisfies a mere lust for power, then such a president will not have an agenda. A person who has no clearly discernible agenda is more dangerous for society than a person who has one, even though he might not disclose it. Someone without an agenda will be swayed in all directions by competing agendas around him.

What is Cyril Ramaphosa's agenda in becoming the president of the ANC and South Africa? Given where the ANC finds itself today, what agenda is possible under the circumstances? The conditions under which Ramaphosa won the ANC presidency are not ideal for him to stamp his authority as leader of the party and as president of the country. He might have won the presidency, but he lost the power play. He was elected through the "fortune of others", as Niccolò Machiavelli argued in *The Prince* (1532). Ramaphosa was carried to victory by a strange coalition of people whose intentions are far from clear. When David Mabuza, now deputy president, threw Ramaphosa a lifeline to win the contest against Nkosazana Dlamini-Zuma, the conditions for this arrangement – this strange victory – were not made clear, at least not to the general public. Could it be that Mabuza has a different agenda for the ANC and for the country?

When I attended the ANC elective conference at Nasrec in December 2017, it dawned on me that South Africa's politics are far more complex than most of us are willing to admit. Viewing the ANC power contest there as a battle between two main factions, the Jacob Zuma faction and the anti-Zuma faction, could no longer help one in analysing what was at play in the ANC. Things had become much more complicated. What I observed at Nasrec was a clear indication that the ANC is moving past factional politics, and that the party is entering the era of interest group politics. It thus becomes important to understand the formation of interest groups within the ANC. Ramaphosa's task ahead of him will be to navigate his way between special interests. This immediately raises the following questions: What's in it for South Africans? What does Nelson Mandela's nation stand to gain or lose as interest groups battle it out in the country? What are the agendas at play?

These questions cannot be answered with absolute certainty, and this book does not claim to give all the answers. But how Ramaphosa will likely come out of all this makes for an interesting discussion. Even more fascinating is how Ramaphosa's skill in managing the competing agendas will impact upon democratic consolidation and economic progress in South Africa. This is the story I aim to tell in this book. Can Ramaphosa pull South Africa out of the quagmire after a decade of corruption and state capture under the Zuma regime? Can Ramaphosa save South Africa, as so many people desperately hope he can? Can he save the ANC? This is no easy task and the odds are stacked against him.

Ramaphosa needs the ANC in order to save South Africa. This means that he firstly has to resuscitate the ANC and get it out of ICU. Only then can he use the party to reach out to South Africans in an attempt to return the nation to its glory days. For Ramaphosa to be successful, the ANC needs to be willing to be saved, even before the nation can be asked to look towards the ANC for solutions to its ills. An ailing ANC which has become resistant to intervention may destroy Ramaphosa's potential to save the country – that is, if we believe he has the potential in the first place. If the ANC refuses assistance from Ramaphosa, then the party will be of no more use to South Africans.

It would be naive to think of the Ramaphosa presidency as an isolated incident or as a "new dawn". Rather, his presidency should be seen as another episode in the evolution of political leadership in post-apartheid South Africa. His presidency has been crafted as an alternative to Zuma's decade of "all things gone wrong". The mere idea that he is an alternative to Zuma implies he is somehow burdened by those years. Up till now, he has had to carefully work his way out of the burden of Zuma. He cannot simply get rid of all those within the ANC who supported Zuma, including some cabinet ministers. If he is seen to be purging Zuma supporters, he will be ousted from the party before the 2019 elections. He has to avoid making enemies.

Diplomacy is an art that Ramaphosa seems to be good at. He speaks eloquently and crafts his messages in a way that seems to give something to everybody. Diplomacy is, however, not the basis for making decisions; it is a way of communicating decisions that are already made. Ramaphosa still needs to make clear what his criteria are for saying yes or no to major policy issues. Thereafter he can go on to diplomatically explain the decisions he has made. President Ramaphosa has to be decisive and stern.

For the first time in post-apartheid South Africa, the ANC is led by someone who has not been in exile or in jail. Does this signal a different leadership culture? If so, what type of leadership style can we expect from Ramaphosa? More interestingly, will his approach to leadership be grounded on the internal logic of the ANC or will he seek to ground his leadership of the ANC in the broader society? Is the ANC ready to embrace a shift in the culture of leadership or will the party resist? The ANC is a hundred-year-old organisation which has passed through many phases, from leading the liberation movement to leading a democratic society. In those years, ANC members have insisted on living up to the traditions of the party, which also entail the idea of "democratic centralism" and discipline among cadres. The ANC has not allowed its leaders to demonstrate personal ambitions above the party.

Ramaphosa's leadership is, however, also an expression of personal ambition. He has a colourful résumé and a depth and range of experience that is unusual: student leader, trade unionist, constitutional negotiator, mining tycoon. In all this, there is evidence of great personal ambition shown by someone who is constantly seeking to influence society by aligning himself with different forces at various points in time. He comes across as adaptable, complex and ambitious. He is not a traditional leader; he is a CV leader. Is the ANC willing to embrace such a man at its head? Judging by his appointment of special "investment envoys" to represent South Africa at the Commonwealth heads of government meeting in London in April 2018, Ramaphosa seems to be more interested in surrounding himself with people who have solid backgrounds. He appointed the market-trusted former finance minister Trevor Manuel and the former finance deputy minister Mcebisi Jonas, famous for refusing to accept a bribe from the Gupta family. The new president topped it with two respected private sector figures, Jacko Maree and Phumzile Langeni. He also appointed the well-known economist Trudi Makhaya as his economic adviser.

Being a product of the ANC could either enhance or damage Ramaphosa's prospects. He took over an ANC that was already divided along ideological lines. He has to manage these divisions and make sure they do not corrode the economy and the state. The ANC that came out of the Nasrec conference has shown an appetite for radical economic policies. If Ramaphosa is unable to get the ANC to scale down on its populism, he will come across as having failed, especially in the eyes of the middle class and the private sector. If he is too successful in curbing the ANC's enthusiasm for radical policies, he will be seen as having betrayed the historical mission of the ANC and abandoned the Freedom Charter. As someone who is understood to be a constitutionalist, Ramaphosa might be called upon to preside over a season of unconstitutional constitutional amendments, should the ANC attempt to amend the Constitution to get its way on policies. If he becomes part of this, Ramaphosa will destroy the reputation he made in constitutional negotiations during the transition to democracy in the early 1990s. If he can protect the Constitution against the ANC, Ramaphosa will cement his reputation as a man of principle.

The aim of this book is to suggest how the story of the presidency of Ramaphosa will unfold. He is a man who says little, and says it well. His eloquence is refreshing, but his ability not to commit to a political position is concerning. This leads me to ask: What type of leadership does South Africa need at this point in time? Do we need someone who has a clear ideological disposition? Or do we need someone who will coordinate action and return the nation to the table for discussions?

I do not believe that South Africa now requires a grand vision shown in the form of an ideology. What I believe is required is someone who can coordinate attempts to clean up the mess we have got into, steer us through the muddle. Ramaphosa is a real coordinator. Will he succeed in coordinating South Africa out of the current impasse?

1.

The Battle of Nasrec

The 54th national conference of the African National Congress (ANC) – held in December 2017 in the Nasrec conference centre in Johannesburg – was the most fiercely and openly contested elective conference yet held in the history of the organisation. The battle that took place here for the soul of the party revealed the worst that could come out of the ANC. Money is reported to have been openly used to persuade members of the branches to vote for particular candidates.[1] *The process of nominating candidates for various leadership positions was marred by deliberate disruption; and in the run-up to the conference court interdicts were issued and physical*

---

1   "ANC vote buying: Mbalula seizes R2.5 million", *Mail & Guardian,* 12 December 2017. Available at: https://mg.co.za/article/2017-12-12-anc-vote-buying-mbalula-seizes-r25-m (accessed 12 December 2017).

intimidation was resorted to, including public displays of violence,[2] at branch, regional and provincial levels of the party. The ANC would never be the same again, nor would South Africans view it and relate to the century-old liberation movement in the same way again.

In the weeks leading up to the Nasrec conference, it was clear that the ANC was in trouble. A growing level of intolerance was evident among party members as they engaged in public spats on the policy direction that the party ought to take. Members traded insults and openly accused one another of hijacking the party for personal gain. The decline in the integrity of the ANC had also divided the party ideologically, and these divisions would later be conveniently exploited by some to pursue factional interests in the party.

The Nasrec conference followed just months after an equally volatile policy conference, which was held in June 2017 at the same venue. When the ANC went into the policy conference, the script that the party sold to the nation emphasised the need for the ANC to engage rigorously on policy so as to enable it to turn the country round and transform the lives of all South Africans, especially the poor and previously disadvantaged. Already at that time, it was public knowledge that former president Jacob Zuma had basically sold the nation to the controversial Gupta family, in the process collecting for himself, his family and cronies some petty cash. The media had just begun publishing the "GuptaLeaks", a series of

---

2   L. Tandwa, "It was a 'festival of chairs': Ramaphosa on violent ANC elective conference", *News24*, 1 October 2017. Available at: https://m.news24.com/SouthAfrica/News/it-was-a-festival-of-chairs-ramaphosa-on-violent-anc-elective-conference-20171001 (accessed 3 October 2017).

revelatory emails detailing how the Gupta family had suborned government ministers, civil servants and even the president himself so as to ensure that lucrative government contracts and tenders were won by or benefited a network of companies associated with or owned by the family.[3]

In the months leading up to Nasrec, things began to unravel for former president Zuma, who faced mounting criticism from members of the ANC alliance namely the Congress of South African Trade Unions (COSATU) and the South African Communist Party (SACP), about his relationship with the Gupta family. Whether the criticism from the alliance partners was based on principle or on mere political expediency no longer matters.

What can be said with certainty is that Zuma betrayed too many people in quick succession, often dumping friends without giving sufficient notice.

By 2017 Zuma's compromised leadership was without any doubt becoming increasingly embarrassing to the party, not to mention the country. Every week the media kept revealing damning new instalments of evidence proving Zuma's involvement in grand corruption.

With his credibility taking a nosedive at a pace never seen before, Zuma fought back. He characterised the negative reports about his leadership as driven by and emanating from so-called white monopoly capital, a term that was widely taken up in the public

---

3   "Here they are: The emails that prove the Guptas run South Africa", *Sunday Times*, 28 May 2017. Available at: https://www.timeslive.co.za/sunday-times/news/2017-05-28-here-they-are-the-emails-that-prove-the-guptas-run-south-africa/ (accessed 2 April 2017).

discourse at the time.[4] In Zuma's version, this racially categorised economic class drew on the support of certain sections of the media and some collaborators within the ANC: a rather improbable alliance. Nevertheless, the term "white monopoly capital" became the subject of intense debates at the June policy conference in 2017.

While the concept of "monopoly capital" had been used by radical, often Marxist academics as far back as the 1970s to characterise the commanding heights of the South African economy under apartheid, its redeployment in recent years turns out to have been engineered by the British PR firm Bell Pottinger, who had been hired by the Gupta family to deflect public criticism from their nefarious business activities.[5] When the term was taken up within the ANC, it led to fierce debates, and ideology came to overlay factional disputes and divisions within the party.

The idea of "white monopoly capital" conveniently brought the justification required to elevate factions, based on personal allegiances to particular leaders, into ideological differences within the party. Perhaps this was inevitable. Factions within political groupings need to make sense of themselves to their affiliate members and to outside observers. If factions can be understood as churches, then ideologies represent faith. There is no strong church without

---

4 G. Makhafola, "White monopoly capital is the enemy, says Zuma", *Independent Online*, 9 June 2017. Available at: https://www.iol.co.za/news/politics/white-monopoloy-capital-is-the-enemy-says-zuma-9687814/ (accessed 10 February 2018).

5 "Dummy's guide: Bell Pottinger – Gupta London agency, creator of WMC", *BizNews*, 7 August. Available at: https://www.google.co.za/amp/s/www.biznews.com/global-citizen/2017/08/07/dummys-guide-bell-pottinger-gupta-wmc/amp/ (accessed 6 September 2017).

a faith; there are no strong factions without ideologies. While members of factions do not usually need much effort to be convinced of the importance and moral basis of their own group, the problem lies with outsiders. They often require a higher level of justification as to why one faction should be seen as more legitimate than another. The factions that existed within the ANC required a much stronger justification for their existence than allegiance to one or other leader. This is where the idea of "white monopoly capital" proved useful, sparking a debate about the necessity or otherwise of radical economic transformation.[6]

At the centre of the debate, however, was a struggle between two dominant factions within the ANC, battling for legitimacy in the public space. On the one side was the anti-Zuma group, which came to occupy the anti-Zuma space that has existed within the party since he took over leadership of the ANC at the 2007 Polokwane conference. This group defined itself against Zuma by assuming an integrity ticket, openly criticising Zuma's leadership for having facilitated what has come to be called state capture. This group was led by Ramaphosa, the deputy president, who successfully managed to remain within Zuma's cabinet while distancing himself from the moral burden of Zuma's wrongdoings and at the same time branding himself apart from and in contradistinction to Zuma, including as an alternative.

Logically, it is difficult to be an alternative to the system that

---

6   G. Sigauqwa, "ANC commission lock horns on monopoly capital", *Mail & Guardian*, 20 December 2017. Available at: https://mg.co.za/article/2017-12-30-anc-commission-lock-horns-on-monopoly-capital (accessed 20 December 2017).

one is part of and serving under. What Ramaphosa did, however, was to create a safe distance between himself and Zuma. When controversial decisions were taken by Zuma, especially those that negatively affected the private sector, Ramaphosa always responded by speaking to the broader context and diluting the strengths of Zuma's position while at the same time opening the matter for further deliberation with more nuances. After Zuma's trusted minerals minister, Mosebenzi Zwane, announced the controversial mining charter in 2017, Ramaphosa quickly moved to allay the fears of the mining industry, distancing himself from the radical charter while opening it up for further negotiations.[7]

In this way Ramaphosa could also ensure that Zuma would appreciate his service of fending off criticisms from what the president perceived as a hostile private sector while at the same time bringing some legitimacy to the policy positions adopted by Zuma by making them the subject of discussion and negotiation with stakeholders. It was a means of creating a win-win situation for both as they took subtle swipes at each other's position while retaining an outward sense of collegiality. This is an example of Ramaphosa's incremental politics, on which I shall elaborate later.

While Ramaphosa was reluctantly assisting the president with some necessary PR work and at the same time nibbling away at Zuma's integrity whenever the opportunity allowed, Zuma pushed the idea that opposition towards his policies were driven by white

7   A. Mbatha and P. Burkhardt, "Ramaphosa says state must negotiate on mine rules", *Moneyweb*, 21 June 2017. Available at: https://www.moneyweb.co. za/news-fast-news/ramaphosa-says-state-must-negotiate-on-mine-rules/ (accessed 2 May 2017).

monopoly capital and its allies within the ANC and civil society. The problem was exacerbated by some of the chief executives in key sectors such as banking and mining, who openly supported Ramaphosa's attempt to spin the most optimistic and positive reading of government policy. Where heroes are scarce, the emergence of a potential saviour such as Ramaphosa inevitably sparks unchecked expressions of enthusiasm. Supporting good people in government is a noble thing and the private sector should not shy away from that. However, writing an open fan letter to an ANC presidential candidate, as one executive did, is not the way to go about it. Some business leaders could simply not hide how smitten they were by Ramaphosa or contain their enthusiasm in showing support for him. This happened both before and after Ramaphosa was elected as ANC president at Nasrec.[8] But by doing so, business leaders in South Africa actually fuelled the anti-establishment sentiment within the ANC. Because of their revolutionary origins and traditions, liberation parties tend to position themselves against mainstream thinking, particularly against capitalism and its ways of doing things. This is equally true of the ANC, which displays in this way its commitment to correcting the capitalist system and the ills of inequality that come with it.

By the time of the ANC policy conference and elective conference at Nasrec in 2017, therefore, there were two extreme positions that divided the ANC. Those on the Zuma side championed the idea of

---

8   A. Haden, "Nedbank CEO offers support to Ramaphosa in open letter", *The South African,* 20 December 2017. Available at: https://www.google.co.za/amp/s/amp.thesouthafrican.com/nedbank-ceo-offers-support-to-rama-phosa-in-open-letter/ (accessed 21 December 2017).

"white monopoly capital" as the strategic enemy of the ANC. On the other side of the divide were those who have been emboldened to advance the idea that the real enemy of progress in South Africa was corruption among ANC members who had compromised the party by serving their own or sectarian interests. The truth of the matter lies in between the extreme postures taken by the two factions. Although Zuma's administration did in fact compromise the integrity of the economy and accelerated corruption, not all problems in South Africa under Zuma could be reducible to corruption. As I demonstrated in my first book, *When Zuma Goes*, there are no leaders within the ANC who can be exonerated from taking collective responsibility for the poor state of affairs that developed within the party and the country. No one within the ANC can claim to be fully beyond reproach. There are differences only in terms of degree of culpability.

Nevertheless, the divisions within the party made for a multi-faceted battle at Nasrec. The conference had both a policy and a leadership battle taking place alongside each other. The leadership battle was fought between former president Zuma's group, with Dlamini-Zuma as their proxy candidate, and the anti-Zuma camp, which ran on an integrity ticket. Ramaphosa emerged as leader of this group, after he faced and fought off challenges from Zweli Mkhize, Lindiwe Sisulu and Mathews Phosa. As I have already mentioned, the anti-Zuma grouping has been in existence as far back as the 2007 Polokwane conference, when Thabo Mbeki lost the leadership battle to Zuma and those who were loyal to Mbeki found themselves out in the cold. Since then, the anti-Zuma camp has taken different forms and has been led by different leaders.

Before Ramaphosa, Kgalema Motlanthe unsuccessfully attempted to topple Zuma at the 2012 Mangaung conference, utilising the anti-Zuma ticket. Ironically, the man who would ascend to power at Nasrec was brought back into politics by Zuma as part of his strategy to repel Motlanthe. But after emerging as the leader of the anti-Zuma group at Nasrec, Ramaphosa soon realised that his camp did not have sufficient power to take him all the way to victory. This was an element of the battle that had to do with leadership and it required a different strategy altogether.

The second element of the battle of Nasrec was the policy battle. It is important to note that when it came to the policy battle, it was the Zuma group that won at Nasrec, with Ramaphosa's group securing only a few disclaimers attached to the end of the policy resolutions that were ultimately adopted by the party. Take, for example, the policy resolution regarding land reform:"Conference resolved that the ANC should, as a matter of policy, pursue expropriation of land without compensation. This should be pursued without destabilising the agricultural sector, without endangering food security in our country and without undermining economic growth and job creation."[9] The first part of the resolution echoes and gives effect to Zuma's project of so-called radical economic transformation. The second part of the resolution, on the other hand, is a disclaimer, a safety valve that will give Ramaphosa the

9 S. Mulholland,"The madness of land expropriation without compensation: Stephen Mulholland unpacks ANC plans", *BizNews*, 28 December 2017. Available at: https://www.google.co.za/amp/s/www.biznews.com/thought-leader/2017/12/28/land-expropriation-stephen-mulholland/amp/ (accessed 28 December 2017).

space to appeal for caution when it comes to setting the pace and scale at which this policy resolution has to be implemented. The rider that the policy of expropriation should "not endanger food security" is a disclaimer that Ramaphosa's supporters can claim as their push-back against radical populism within the party. Such a compromise must surely paralyse the party: it is still not clear whether the basic thrust of the policy should be to avoid endangering food security by all means or to fast-track land reform while making sure that only acceptable impairments of food security are allowed. The reality is that policies often produce some level of unwanted results. The question is what level of collateral damage is acceptable, and according to whose standard. As it turned out, Nasrec could not resolve the policy squabbles within the ANC. The conference only further institutionalised the long-standing divisions within the party in the form of policy resolutions.

On policy matters, neither of the factions that went into the Nasrec conference could claim an outright victory. When it came to the leadership battle, at least the party presidential race, there was a clear winner. Ramaphosa can be said to have won. However, his victory did not come about in the way in which it was expected. I am convinced that because of a great sense of yearning for leadership change following the Zuma era, South Africans are not willing to appreciate the complexity of the leadership battle that ensued at Nasrec and the manner in which it was decided. True indeed, Ramaphosa won sufficient votes to become the president of the ANC. However, his supporters within the party did not ascend with him to the top positions. It became a very lonely victory as Ramaphosa emerged the winner but found himself surrounded by some very hostile forces. This was a far cry from the hope that Rama-phosa's victory would represent a clean sweep of the party, indica-tive of deep changes effected within the ANC.

In the run-up to the elective conference in 2017, various institu-tions carried out monthly surveys of the unfolding contest between Ramaphosa and Dlamini-Zuma. Throughout this time, I main-tained that while Ramaphosa dominated the narratives in the broader public discourse, Dlamini-Zuma was actually in the lead. Most of my colleagues disagreed with me, and they were proved correct. Of concern for me was that, though probably correct, they underestimated the infrastructure and resource base of the Zuma camp and overestimated the likely success of what was a relatively weak campaign pursued by Ramaphosa. It seemed to me that the chances that Ramaphosa would win the race by relying solely on the anti-Zuma support base were very slim.

In fact, Ramaphosa's victory came about through a strange com-bination of contradictory agendas knitted together in the eleventh hour with the sole purpose of securing a particular set of leadership results. Since neither faction, the Zuma or the anti-Zuma grouping, held an outright majority, the contest was won by an interest group that managed to subsume and overwhelm both factions. Unlike the two dominant factions within the party, it was the so-called Premier League – comprising former North West premier Supra Mahumapelo, Mpumalanga premier David Mabuza and Free State premier Ace Magashule – that came out of Nasrec with the maximum returns possible. In this way they outsmarted both the Zuma and the anti-Zuma factions, which had entered the conference with firm and uncompromising agendas. The Premier League was more than a faction; it was an interest group capable of exploiting either of the factions that existed. And it exhibited a resolute determination to win the leadership contest, which it in fact did.

The success of the Premier League has fuelled speculation, especially among the two factions, that Nasrec was rigged. There was a strong feeling at the conference that the results of the conference were fiddled with and adjusted, and as a result there were demands for recounts after the results came in.[10] One must bear in mind, however, that the suspicion of rigging had been there in the period leading up to the conference. The provincial and regional conferences of the party responsible for preparing the branches for the national conference faced numerous disputes relating to processes of selection and election.

But whatever the truth of these allegations, there is no doubt in my mind that the outcomes of the elections were engineered by the Premier League, particularly in deciding the pecking order of the top six positions. In reaction to former president Zuma's stubborn resolve to impose Dlamini-Zuma as his faction's candidate, the Premier League's power broker, David Mabuza, began to consider packing the top leadership of the ANC with people of his own choice. Had Zuma been more democratic and amicable when it came to deciding who was the rightful bearer of the torch for the Zuma camp, the conference could have turned out very differently. Instead, Mabuza gauged the power play by both the Ramaphosa and Zuma factions and arrived at the conclusion that he could

---

10 "Supporters of Dlamini Zuma may legally appeal the results of the ANC conference", *The Citizen*, 19 December 2017.

maximise his returns from the conference by playing both factions against each other, weakening them individually and thereby strengthening his position as leader of an interest group. Mabuza realised that Ramaphosa was useful as the president because of his integrity and his ability to help the party win the 2019 general elections. At the same time, Mabuza did not openly state his reservations about supporting Dlamini-Zuma because this would have alienated Zuma, who would have used all the means at his disposal to stymie Mabuza.

Although Ramaphosa waged a morally superior campaign, he still did not have a winning plan. Put differently, Ramaphosa did not have a solid strategy to stop other contenders from winning. In the end, Ramaphosa owed his victory to Mabuza, who elevated him to a winning position that his own poorly performing faction could not have delivered. When the deed was done, the Dlamini-Zuma faction was left in shock and surprise, crying betrayal after realising that Mabuza used them, neutralised them, and also engineered the appointments of the top six leaders. As for the Ramaphosa faction, they simply put on a brave face.

Now that he has weakened the Zuma faction and secured the kind of victory he preferred – standing beside the respectable Ramaphosa instead of the compromised Dlamini-Zuma – Mabuza is probably already thinking beyond the Premier League. It has been murmured in media circles that Mabuza despises the manner in which Zuma embarrassed himself in the revelations about state capture. This is seen as the reason why Mabuza reportedly shunned Dlamini-Zuma's candidature. Perhaps what it boils down to in the end is that Mabuza opposes the Gupta monopoly on corruption.

The result of the Nasrec battle reveals the complexity of the contradicting agendas that have seized control of the party. Beyond the factions, there are powerful and dangerous interests groups that have gained the upper hand in the ANC. Interest groups are more focused than factions, and they can exist across factions. They are also very adaptable. Furthermore, the politics of interest groups can be more damaging to democracy than haphazard factions. The question that is important to address is how the ANC as a party will proceed in addressing the priorities such as poverty and unemployment, given the proliferation of special interest and factionalism within the party.

Looking at the battle of Nasrec, we should ask how the ANC will carry on in its attempt to consolidate power and avoid losing the 2019 elections. What does Nasrec say about the need for the party to be firm and resolute against corruption? What does Nasrec signify for the policy directions that will be taken by the ANC in the future, and how will opposition parties respond to all this? Ramaphosa's presidency will have to deal with the interest group politics that have emerged from Nasrec. This is a difficult battle. But with his history of straddling different groups and navigating his way through competing interests, perhaps Ramaphosa will demonstrate his prowess as he steers the party into the future.

2.

The Real Cyril Ramaphosa

Cyril Ramaphosa has had an enormously impressive and varied experience of public leadership. As someone who has come through the radical student movement that emphasised the plight of black students under apartheid; served within the trade union movement and facilitated its links with the broader social movement; searched for and found consensus during South Africa's negotiations for democracy; built a relationship with the business community; and then quietly returned to politics, ending up as deputy president and then president of the country, Ramaphosa has truly seen it all. With all this experience under his belt, Ramaphosa may be the most well-equipped and capable leader to run the ANC and the country in the post-apartheid era.

After matriculating from Mphaphuli High School, which pro-duced the leading students in what was then the homeland of

Venda (now part of Limpopo province), Ramaphosa attended what was then called the University of the North (or Turfloop) to study law. Here he became involved in the student movement, both the Student Christian Movement and Black Consciousness. Professor Malegapuru Makgoba, who has worked with Ramaphosa in the National Planning Commission, says of him, "Cyril is SASO." The South African Students Organisation, founded in the late 1960s by Steve Biko and other proponents of Black Consciousness, became the embodiment of intellectual self-determination among black students who wanted to play a decisive role in the struggle against apartheid. According to Biko,[11] Black Consciousness was a way to ground the anti-apartheid movement in the lived experience of black students. It was an affirmation of black identity as a tool to contest the political, social, economic and cultural subjugation of black people. Here within SASO Ramaphosa cut his teeth as a leader.

After completing his studies, Ramaphosa began work in the trade union movement, and in 1982 helped found the National Union of Mineworkers (NUM),[12] whose first secretary he became. NUM developed into a powerful union in the mining sector and became an indomitable anti-apartheid force on the labour front. In the fight against apartheid, economic disruptions in the form of labour strikes inflicted serious harm on the system, and helped turn the captains of industry and the economic establishment against the National Party and the system of apartheid.

11 S. Biko, *I Write What I Like*. London: Bowerdean Press, 1978.
12 National Union of Mineworkers, "NUM history". Available at: https://num.com/company/history/ (accessed 2 February 2018).

NUM and Ramaphosa were subsequently instrumental in the formation of the trade union federation COSATU, which was launched in December 1985 and whose general secretary Ramaphosa became.[13] The mining sector, which had been built up historically on the back of the exploitative migrant labour system, would provide a good arena for COSATU to link labour practices in South Africa with the broader struggle for social justice. COSATU was not an ordinary union focused only on the narrow shopfloor interests of workers; it built solidarity with other social movements outside the labour sector such as civil society, the churches, political organisations and student movements. COSATU's strength was its mass appeal: under Ramaphosa's leadership, union membership grew from 6,000 in 1982 to 300,000 in 1992, giving it control of nearly half of the total black workforce in the South African mining industry. Some trade union historians speak of COSATU as an example of "mass movement trade unionism",[14] and correctly so. This is the reason why most of those who led COSATU were also linked to the broader grassroots movement against apartheid, represented nationally by the United Democratic Front (UDF). It was through the mass anti-apartheid movement that Ramaphosa emerged as a leader on the national stage.

The UDF, formed in Cape Town in 1983, was an umbrella organi-

---

13   COSATU, "Brief history of COSATU". Available at: http://www.cosatu.org. za/show.php?ID=925 (accessed 15 February 2018).

14   T. Bramble, "Social movement unionism since the fall of apartheid: The case of NUMSA on the East Rand", in T. Bramble and F. Barchiesi (eds), *Rethinking the Labour Movement in the "New South Africa"*. Ashgate: Aldershot, 2003.

sation drawing together hundreds of youth movements, community organisations, trade unions, professional bodies and church groups throughout the country. When both the UDF and COSATU came under increasing government restrictions in the late 1980s, the two came together to cooperate in a loose alliance called the Mass Democratic Movement (MDM), in which Ramaphosa took a leading role. Ramaphosa's own story needs to be understood within the context of the "grassroots coalition"[15] that resulted in mass resistance against the apartheid system. If Ramaphosa's ascent to power as president of the ANC and of the country is an indication of a shift in leadership approach, the politics of the UDF and MDM offer a good starting point for understanding what this shift might entail. It is from this vantage point that Ramaphosa's leadership style should be understood.

Led organically by a group of local activists within the country, the UDF/MDM produced a breed of leaders who navigated between the ANC's Marxist revolutionary politics and the practical limitations of operating within the country under an oppressive system. Historians agree that the UDF was "an amalgam of rather diverse organisations over which the central leadership exerted only a loose control".[16] Mass movements that operate outside a formal institutional framework tend to be loosely organised and lack a

---

15   J.B. Spector, "The UDF at 30: An organisation that shook apartheid's foundation", *Daily Maverick*, 22 August 2013. Available at: https://www.daily-maverick.co.za/article/2013-08-22-the-udf-at-30-an-organisation-that-shook-apartheids-foundation/#.WpFgn-huY2w (accessed 13 October 2017).

16   J. Seekings, *The UDF: A History of the United Democratic Front in South Africa 1983–1991*. Cape Town: David Philip, 2000.

centralised leadership and system of command. Unlike political parties, they often do not subscribe to a hierarchical structure. The UDF displayed a democratic culture typical of mass movements, demonstrating a haphazard organisational life and lack of coordinated leadership. The leadership style of the UDF was dominated by the notion of collective leadership, very unlike the ANC's idea of democratic centralism. All in all, the UDF produced a breed of leaders with a distinct culture of leadership that was shaped by the immediate circumstances under which the movement then existed. It is within this context that Ramaphosa's leadership style developed.

Judged in terms of a hierarchical pattern of leadership, with systematic and clearly defined flows of power from leaders to members, the UDF did not fare well. From the bureaucratic point of view, it was poorly constituted. But when it came to its ability to inspire the masses to take political action, the UDF was exceptionally effective in undermining the apartheid system. It was because of the success of the UDF's internal resistance that the apartheid government lost the capacity to control the country in the eyes of the international community and its own followers.[17] As a result of the disruptions caused by the UDF, it became difficult for the apartheid government to assure the regime's increasingly jittery allies that the situation in South Africa was in hand. For those who sympathised with the UDF, on the other hand, the formation raised

17 S. Kleiner, "Apartheid amnesia: How the GOP conveniently forgot about its role in propping up a white supremacist regime", *Foreign Policy*, 19 July 2013. Available at: http://foreignpolicy.com/2013/07/19/apartheid-amnesia/ (accessed 10 October 2017).

the hope that apartheid could be defeated without violence – by the staging of public protests and labour stay-aways. These were the manoeuvres that exposed the hollowness of the regime's PR campaign and undermined the piecemeal reforms that the regime sought to undertake to defuse tensions in the country.

Today there are many prominent leaders in South Africa with roots in the UDF. They are currently found throughout the population: in churches, the business sector, civil society, universities, government, trade unions and political parties alike. When the ANC was unbanned in 1990 and the democratic transition began in the country, most of the UDF leaders invoked their membership of the ANC. On their return to South Africa, the formerly exiled leaders of the ANC displaced the local UDF leaders and ensured that their own people would take centre stage in the political leadership of the country. It would also mean that the party would practise a type of leadership that had been learned in exile, particularly from countries in the Soviet bloc.

From a moral point of view, the UDF could not press for its continued existence once the ANC had returned. This was because it seemed morally indefensible for any organisation to attempt to compete with the majestic ANC, which had been in exile for decades and accumulated enormous international respect and credibility. The euphoria that surrounded the prospect and then the reality of an ANC-led democratic government was so powerful that there was no space for proper consideration of the future of the UDF. Mass driven as it was, the UDF could not compete with the ANC, and hence the organisation was disbanded and its members joined the ranks of the ANC and other parties in the country. The

UDF as a political idea became frozen, only to make a return with the ANC's decline of legitimacy later in the process of democratic consolidation in the country.

Ramaphosa's return to politics is part of this gradual process of unfreezing of the UDF principles of leadership and mobilisation. Indeed, by rejecting Zuma and his allies and electing Ramaphosa at Nasrec in 2017, ANC members may have unintentionally opened the way for a return of the leadership tradition of the UDF.

Quite often when people reflect retrospectively on the UDF in post-apartheid South Africa, those reflections are nostalgic and tend to call for the re-establishment of the UDF as a mass-based movement. But there may no longer be space for a mass movement like the UDF in the current South Africa, simply because organised political parties are generally accepted as the best way for conducting politics in modern democracies. As Dominika Kruszewska notes, "because democracy requires organisation, mass movements face pressure to create formal organisations to successfully advance their goals".[18] As a disruptor of the apartheid system, the UDF was perfect in this sense. But in a democratic society, the movement would not be able to serve as a platform for pursuing political goals. After the great sea change of the early 1990s, either the UDF had to be organised into a formal political party or it had to disperse.

Why is the UDF so important in understanding Ramaphosa's leadership? This has much to do with his role and ability as a co-

---

18   D. Kruszewska, "Social movements and political parties", *Harvard Projects*. Available at: http://projects.iq.harvard.edu/files/mobilized_contention/files/movementsandparties.pdf (accessed 4 November 2017).

ordinator. According to Makgoba, each of South Africa's post-1994 presidents has embodied a different leadership style. Former president Zuma was a political survivor and his leadership style lacked the grand vision that Nelson Mandela, for instance, exhibited. Mandela's brand of leadership was, on the contrary, able to unite people behind the vision of a multiracial prosperous South Africa. Yet, in the event, Mandela did not deliver significantly in terms of substantive matters and lacked the ability to coordinate action towards the achievement of his grand vision.

According to Makgoba, Ramaphosa can best be understood as a coordinator; more specifically, a consensus-driven coordinator. Citing his experience of working with Ramaphosa at the National Planning Commission, of which Ramaphosa was deputy chairperson, Makgoba pointed to the commission's achievements under Ramaphosa's leadership: first of all the diagnostic report and then the National Development Plan (NDP). I have misgivings about long-term grand plans, particularly for a country which is suffering from basic problems of state capacity and functional bureaucracy.[19] But compared with other grand policy positions that have been adopted by the ANC government since 1994, the NDP has attracted a great degree of consensus. Even the opposition Democratic Alliance has said: "The National Planning Commission's National Development Plan (NDP) points to an emerging consensus at the non-racial, progressive centre of South African politics. The developing policy coherence on the fundamental issues facing South

---

19   R. Mathekga, *When Zuma Goes*. Cape Town: Tafelberg, 2016.

Africa is an exciting and significant development."[20] The process of drafting and adopting the NDP was arguably one of the few political processes that involved multi-stakeholder approaches, as is evident from the wide buy-in from key interests, parties and organisations in the country. It is indeed compelling to look at the plan as an attempt at a consensus-driven approach to forming a coordinated grand vision for South Africa.

Beside all the other things he has accomplished, including his work on the NDP, Ramaphosa also led the process of negotiations that produced the Constitution of South Africa in 1996. In recent years, radical young South Africans, particularly members of the Economic Freedom Fighters (EFF), have tended to denounce the Constitution as a sham, a Judas Iscariot moment when the revolution was sold for a few pieces of silver. This is the explanation they advance whenever they are frustrated with the slow pace of progress in post-apartheid South Africa. Yet in reality the negotiations were not an easy path and they also came close to shipwreck on several occasions. In the end, consensus was arrived at and the principles laid out then have shaped the political system till today.

When opening the CODESA (Convention for a Democratic South Africa) talks in 1991, Mandela remarked: "The diverse interests represented [here] speak of the capacity to develop consensus across the spectrum and of the desire to maximise common purpose

---

20 Democratic Alliance, "The National Development Plan: An emerging progressive consensus", 23 November 2013. Available at: https://www.da.org.za/archive/the-national-development-plan-an-emerging-progressive-consensus/ (accessed 1 February 2018).

amongst South Africans."[21] Mandela had a clear sense that it would take a great deal of concession on all sides for the talks to yield a united front amid conflicting interests. As Professor Shadrack Gutto used to emphasise to us students at the Wits Law School, strong consensus occurs when all or most parties agree on the main issues, not necessarily on everything. It is the willingness to gain some and let go of some. Consensus does not produce losers and winners; rather, it produces a common front and a common commitment to defend the outcomes publicly. During the negotiations for South Africa's transition, it was Ramaphosa's duty as the leading negotiator for the ANC to secure consensus, and secure it he did.

Now with hindsight, particularly after the Zuma era has passed, we can see the wisdom of what was achieved with the negotiations: the values of the Constitution have become deeply infused into the political system that we inhabit. Even the EFF, with its ambivalence towards the Constitution, anchored its successful bid to frustrate Zuma on the basis of the very Constitution. Moreover, Zuma's resistance to criticism and his resort to court actions were also anchored on the very same Constitution: he often bemoaned the fact that his constitutional rights as president and as an individual had been violated. As has been remarked, some of the best developments in our society have come about through people with the most sinister motives.

In the post-Zuma era, the South Africa we have today requires a

---

21 ANC, "CODESA: Opening statement by Nelson Mandela president of the ANC", 20 December 1991. Available at: http://www.anc.org.za/content/codesa-opening-statement-nelson-mandela-anc (accessed 9 January 2018).

different approach in terms of political leadership. One hopes that Ramaphosa will indeed fit the bill and prove capable of leading this complex multicultural, democratic society. With all his experience, as we have outlined in this chapter, Ramaphosa is well qualified and equipped to lead the ANC and the country at this point in time. In many previous stages of his life, he demonstrated that he could improvise and adapt to different contexts and the demands of different institutions with varying organisational cultures. He has emerged from his history as coordinator-in-chief: the coordinator of consensus.

For the first time in post-apartheid history, the ANC is now led by someone who did not go into exile. This also says that Ramaphosa knows how to operate within a system, while most ANC members who were in exile only observed systems without necessarily participating in them. In exile, the idea of leadership was formed in abstraction, by way of observing and reading and not by participation. Here at home during the last few years of apartheid, oppositional leadership had to contend with the practicality of functioning within the constraints of apartheid, a system nonetheless. What are the positive aspects that accrue to individuals who learn to function within a system, even when they are politically excluded by the system? In leading movements that had to navigate through the apartheid system, Ramaphosa had to appeal to the idea of consensus, as the best way to keep everyone believing that change would come. In a similar manner, democracy is also a game of confidence. If people have confidence in the system because they believe it has potential, they tend to see solutions instead of problems.

Ramaphosa's return to politics could signal a different agenda from the one that has been pursued by the ANC in recent years. The question is whether he will resuscitate the consensus approach to politics and, if so, what the role of the EFF will be. It is not clear what Ramaphosa's key agenda is. He is a complex leader with an incredible ability to adapt to organisations and circumstances. He also carries the legitimacy of having led mass movements, an un-disputed currency in South Africa's culture of mass mobilisation. South Africans tend to believe that, while you can win over the table through quiet negotiations, you can do even better if you march on the streets and disrupt other people from going about their lives. That's Ramaphosa's people for you.

3.

Leading a Fragmented Nation

―⁓―

Ramaphosa's campaign for the leadership of the ANC was partially organised and managed from outside ANC party structures. It is significant that it was the first time in the history of leadership succession in the ANC that a candidate enjoyed greater support and legitimacy from outside the party than from within. At times during the build-up to the ANC elective conference held in December 2017, one could easily have concluded that Ramaphosa was campaigning for the presidency of the country, and not of the ANC.

The campaign that was built up around Ramaphosa was packaged as an integrity ticket. It presented ANC members an opportunity to choose a leader who sought to re-ground the ANC within society. If successful, this project would see the ANC shifting from an inward-looking organisation towards a party grounded on broader societal values shared widely outside. This has deep and serious implications for how Ramaphosa will most likely lead the party and the country. While he will depend on allies from within and outside the ANC, his leadership style will be grounded on broader values shared by a wide spread of people outside the ANC. If the ANC had drifted away from the people under the leadership of Thabo Mbeki and Jacob Zuma, then Ramaphosa's accession to power was an attempt to bring the party closer to the people.

If the ANC still wishes to continue to lead the country, it will need to adapt and learn to appreciate the value system that is shared and demonstrated by the broader society. This means that the ANC will have to justify its moral claim to leadership of the country by looking beyond party membership. Despite numerous attempts to modernise the ANC[22] and ensure that it reflects the values and complexity of the society it leads – a post-liberation market society with a vast backlog of social deficits – the party still needs to ground itself partially, if not wholly, within the very society it seeks to lead.

Since its return from exile and taking over political leadership of the country, the ANC has been battling to position itself as more than a liberation movement. To demonstrate its diversity in terms of membership, and by implication the breadth of its political agenda, ANC members often assert that the party is "a broad church for all".[23] Nevertheless, the manner in which the ANC carries itself

---

22   W. Gumede, "Modernising the African National Congress: The legacy of President Thabo Mbeki", in P. Kagwanja and K. Kwandile (eds), *State of the Nation: South Africa 2008*. Cape Town: HSRC Press, 2009.

23   See ANC 50th National Conference Discussion Document.

shows that the party has thus far been inward-looking in its understanding of its identity and in its approach to leadership of the country, and that it struggles to connect with broader societal values. The ANC often justifies its conduct and action on the basis of an inwardly developed agenda consistent with its role of a liberation movement guided by such historically defined goals as the liberation of black people from all forms of colonialism and oppression.[24] In this way, the ANC appears parochial and only concerned with its historical constituents, which are narrowly defined as the poor black working class. Its main objective is to reinstate those who were previously excluded from political and economic participation in society under the apartheid system. This is the basis from which the ANC draws its moral authority to lead.

The question then arises: what happens when the party can no longer appeal to its historical constituents by using the historical justifications based on the effects of apartheid on society? This is not to argue that the society is becoming blind to the historical impact of apartheid. It is one thing for the legacies of apartheid to be still visible on the ground; it is quite another for such effects to provide a basis for justifying a political project in an open, democratic society. Apartheid identities were essentially exclusive. Thus, black was defined to exclude white, and vice versa. Therefore, a solution that seeks to target this historical problem by appealing strictly to those historical identities will end up entrenching those

---

24   "What is the African National Congress?" Available at: http://www.anc.org.
za/content/what-anc.

identities and appear to be based on exclusion: the very historical challenge it seeks to remedy.

In the meantime, South Africa has evolved to the point where the effects of apartheid no longer serve as sufficient justification for a political project in the country. What is needed instead are innovative policy remedies to historical challenges such as inequality. Failure to pay heed to this will limit the party's growth in a modern society. Even worse, many South Africans have remarked that the apartheid government was better organised than the ANC-led government.[25] This is often an expression of frustration with the shortfalls of the democratic system, particularly when it comes to the effectiveness of the bureaucracy in carrying out basic functions and delivering services to the people. For example, it is often stated as fact that the education system under apartheid was far better than what is experienced in post-apartheid South Africa.[26] This is not true: the post-apartheid education system is in fact better than apartheid's Bantu Education system.[27] Such remarks are common ways of expressing frustration with poorly implemented education policies in a democratic South Africa. Historical

---

25 "South Africans say life was better before ANC took over: Poll", *Business-Tech*, 27 April 2016. Available at: https://businesstech.co.za/news/government/121636/south-africans-say-life-was-better-before-anc-took-over-poll/ (accessed 12 February 2017).

26 "Education system worse than under apartheid: Ramphele", *Mail & Guardian*, 23 March 2012. Available at: https://mg.co.za/article/2012-03-23-education-system-worse-than-under-apartheid-ramphele (accessed 10 February 2017).

27 A. Nyoka, E. du Plooy and S. Hanekom, "Reconciliation for South Africa's education system", *Elm Magazine*, 25 June 2014. Available at: http://www.elmmagazine.eu/articles/reconciliation-for-south-africa-s-education-system/ (accessed 24 January 2017).

challenges such as inequality, which have their roots in the apartheid system, remain endemic and therefore a source of political rallying in South Africa. It is what keeps the EFF relevant, because the democratic dispensation has been unable to address this impasse. In the longer term, however, as South Africa evolves and gathers more experience in experimenting with democracy, historical factors such as these will lose their impetus as a basis for justifying political action and political leadership.

At the same time, as South Africa becomes an increasingly complex society, political parties will need to craft correspondingly complex political projects to lead society. This applies not only to the ANC. The Democratic Alliance (DA) follows a similar approach to that of the ANC by focusing on the interests of whites as its core constituents. Within the DA, blacks are often regarded simply as an electoral strategy, not as an integral part of an evolving identity that will enable the party to adapt to a complex society. It is in this sense that both the ANC and the DA have political identities that are inward-looking, focusing on how each historically understands its place and role in South Africa, while at large the country is rapidly shifting away from this mode of understanding and grounding leadership. The two parties are merely two sides of the same coin: an apartheid-minted coin which is losing its shine.

Consider, for example, how the ANC often handles its relations with the black middle class in the country. Those who enter this category through some form of social and economic mobility automatically become an irritant to the ANC since they are no longer catered for by the party's stagnant identity based on its historical role as a liberation movement. The middle class, or the "clever blacks,"[28] were the first group of people to fall out with the ANC, migrating to parties such as the Congress of the People (COPE) and the DA, where they felt more at home.

It was also not by accident that some outspoken ANC members have found refuge outside the party, predominantly within civil society, a space where soundness and common sense prevail. The formation of the Save South Africa[29] movement, for instance, is a clear indication of how members of the party are seeking to craft a basis for leadership by looking outside. Made up of disgruntled ANC members who experienced displacement under Zuma's embarrassing version of African leadership, Save South Africa was an attempt to re-ground leadership by relocating its moral basis outside the ANC. The message of Save South Africa was that the ANC had been hijacked by Zuma and his allies. Therefore, the best way to save the ANC was to forge a platform outside the party, upon which to reclaim the moral ground for leadership. This is the group that supported Ramaphosa, who himself decided to rebuild the ANC from the outside while remaining on the inside.

Of the two groups at the centre of power within the ANC, the Zuma group rejected any attempt to re-ground the ANC in the broader society. They did not approve of any measure to bring external sources of justification into the party. These are the people who drove the anti-establishment sentiments within the ANC,

---

28 Reference used by former president Jacob Zuma in his address to the National House of Traditional Leaders in 2012.

29 The Save South Africa campaign was launched in response to a growing number of people who were concerned about the increase in corruption, the looting of state resources and the undermining of the Constitution.

rejecting anything approved of in the mainstream society. Their approach is reflected in the common retort by the ANC that the party cannot be dictated to by other people as to how it should run its own affairs.

The logic is that if something makes sense to the ANC internally as a party, then it does not necessarily have to make sense to the broader society. The message is that the ANC will not bother to find out why the party finds itself far removed from society when it comes to handling contentious issues such as the upgrades to Zuma's private residence at Nkandla. As a result, the ANC was isolated on this issue from the broader mass of society in its insistence that Zuma did not need to pay back a portion of the taxpayers' money spent on the renovation of his private home, as the Public Protector, Advocate Thuli Madonsela, had ordered him to do.

The evidence for this isolation of the ANC from the broader society had been steadfastly piling up during Zuma's tenure of office since 2009. But the problem stretches far back, even to the Mbeki era, when under the direction of the president, the ANC government refused to roll out antiretrovirals to treat the HIV/AIDS pandemic, despite the public outcry.

The problem can also be seen in the extreme form of nationalism that has engulfed the party, when it seeks self-determination – "African solutions" – even on matters that are universally agreed upon. Then, too, there are those within the ANC who believe that whenever the party's conduct or leadership conflicts with constitutional principles, this is an indication that there is something wrong with the Constitution.[30] Seldom does the ANC reflect on its policies or conduct with the aim of finding ways in which they can be grounded upon constitutional principles and the values that are widely shared in the broader society.

In the recent contest for leadership of the party, Cyril Ramaphosa's campaign was a direct challenge to the ANC's traditional ways of thinking. While his opponent, Nkosazana Dlamini-Zuma, whose campaign was firmly located within the party, lost the contest to lead the ANC, Ramaphosa's victory does not mean that his project to ground the ANC in the broader society was universally approved by the wider ANC membership. I believe there are strong sentiments within the ANC to retain an inward-looking approach to leadership. By rejecting Ramaphosa's power backers and his slate, which enjoyed widespread approval and legitimacy outside the party, the ANC has attempted to impose constraints on Ramaphosa's leadership. For instance, had his wish been granted, Ramaphosa would have served alongside Lindiwe Sisulu as his deputy president. No matter at what speed the Ramaphosa train travels, it will still have to move along the tracks laid down by the party.

As mentioned earlier, Ramaphosa's leadership style differs from the liberation movement approach and tends towards a more broad-based, consultative style. In this style, the justification for political conduct is more broadly based than on the dictates of the party and involves wider consultation with the people. In this regard, it

---

30 G. Nicolson, "Land, actually: What's the ANC's policy?", *Daily Maverick*, 6 March 2017. Available at: https://www.dailymaverick.co.za/article/2017-03-06-land-actually-whats-the-ancs-policy/#.Woh7gaiWY2w (accessed 15 October 2017).

is significant that whereas Zuma went into exile, Ramaphosa never did. Thus, while Zuma drew legitimacy for his leadership from the moral basis of exile politics, which historically remained contained and organised within the party, Ramaphosa would derive legitimacy for his decisions and leadership, particularly in the 1980s and early 1990s, from the political culture of mass activism.

Exiled liberation political parties tend to justify their actions on the basis of a shared value system crafted by party insiders and sold to members as the gospel. This moral basis for the party's struggle proved effective in fighting against colonialism and repressive regimes such as apartheid, but it has failed dismally to serve as a basis for justification in newly liberated nations.

Problems emerge during the period of democratic consolidation when liberation parties continue to operate as exclusive entities focused only on the narrow interests of those who have been liberated, forgetting that liberation also entails liberating even those who benefited from the former oppressive regime. Moreover, once liberation is attained, the expectations of the broader population place new demands on the liberation movement and its style of leadership, even if there are not major improvements in the material conditions of the majority of people or they are slow in coming. Liberation parties fall short in this regard, and tend to lag behind society, leading from behind.

Citizens have two sets of demands from a state, and those demands may be compatible or contradictory, depending on historical conditions. The first set of demands has to do with the health of political interactions, including accountability by those who exercise power.[31] The second set of demands has to do with the material returns of democracy as a system of distributing or redistributing resources and opportunities. This has been the subject of concern both politically and philosophically. Besides offering healthy and dynamic engagements for people, democracy should bring about material changes in people's living conditions. In a well-functioning democracy, people should have access to running water, basic amenities, education and employment, for example. These are the material benefits that are associated with an optimal society. Democracy should also provide people with an open environment in which they can exchange ideas, formulate political choices and then exercise them. Poor people are just as much entitled to a lively dynamic democracy as they are to improved living conditions.

Once an oppressive regime has been defeated, poor people may find the language and discourse of liberation parties increasingly monotonous and devoid of imagination. The poor have a right to reject the single-track approach of liberation politics pursued by liberation parties in democratic dispensations such as South Africa. The ANC's approach to leadership has been to craft a simple message about the poor and then package it as a moral justification for its decisions. There seems to be a common view that says that the poor are inherently unsophisticated and uninterested in demanding things such as good governance because they are only concerned with access to basic necessities. This is not the case. The poor in South Africa also had a problem with Zuma's liberation

---

31 See the German philosopher Jürgen Habermas's work on communicative rationality and the public sphere.

politics, particularly the manner in which it failed to meet the required standards of justification and accountability required by the broader society.

As we can now see, Ramaphosa is confronted with both risks and opportunities when it comes to leading the country. The risks he faces are those within the ANC, while there are opportunities galore outside the party. The question is: how will he navigate this minefield as he crafts his leadership style? He has to manage the internal expectations among his comrades within the ANC while at the same time ensuring that he meets the broader requirements of justification demanded by the wider society. Distinguishing between the ANC and the broader society is not meant to say that the ANC does not exist within society. There are distinct moral bases for leadership within the ANC, and within the broader society outside the ANC. Ramaphosa has one foot in the ANC by virtue of the fact that he is the president of the organisation, and another foot in the broader society in the sense that he enjoys wider legitimacy outside the ANC as president of the country.

The risk is that whenever Ramaphosa brings to the ANC a justification that comes from outside, he will face resistance from within the party. Having run an outward-looking campaign to lead the ANC, Ramaphosa is widely seen as a threat by those who are set on retaining the liberation character of the ANC and its inward-looking basis for leadership. These are the people who genuinely believe that the ANC is under threat from a takeover or destabilisation by outside elements. Whenever the ANC is pushed into a corner, the party has a habit of alleging conspiracy by hostile foreign elements aimed at undermining the party's progressive agenda as the oldest liberation movement on the continent. That is how the ANC rejects the level of accountability demanded by the broader society, by relying on loyalty to the party's character as a liberation party.[32] Whether or not the people behind this kind of thinking genuinely believe this does not matter. What matters is that the problem itself has become genuine, and it has implications for how Ramaphosa will lead the ANC and the country.

The greatest risk that Ramaphosa faces is that in his attempt to show the ANC the way, he will be accused of capturing it and selling it to his friends in the business sector who masquerade as representatives of the public interest. Ramaphosa can insist that all he is trying to do is show the ANC how it can ground itself in the broader society. He can further assure the party that he wants to secure its position in history as the first liberation party to adapt to a modern democratic system. This is the case Ramaphosa can take to the ANC jury, hoping he will be allowed to recreate a good relationship between the party and the broader society. For some within the ANC, however, this is just a plausible sales pitch: something Ramaphosa is certainly known for.

Whatever decision he makes as president of the country, Ramaphosa has to consider the extent to which it will offend some within the ANC, particularly when the decision is in the outright interests of the broader society and justifiable outside the ANC. It looks like he is heeding this advice, as his first cabinet reshuffle in February

---

32   R. Mathekga, "On sovereignty: SA is its own worst enemy", *News24*, 10 July 2017. Available at: https://www.news24.com/Columnists/Ralph_Mathekga/ on-sovereignty-sa-is-its-own-worst-enemy-20170710 (accessed 10 November 2017).

2018 seems to indicate. He managed to get rid of some ministers he inherited from Zuma, particularly those who occupied key positions such as finance, public enterprises and foreign affairs. By doing so, he yielded to common sense outside the ANC and the common feeling that he should stamp his authority when it comes to key departments at the forefront of government policy. At the same time, to ensure that he did not totally abandon the ANC line, Ramaphosa retained in his cabinet some of the ministers known to be Zuma loyalists and implicated in maladministration in the Zuma years. The controversial Malusi Gigaba was retained, although demoted to minister of home affairs. The controversial ANC Women's League president, Bathabile Dlamini, was kept on but moved to a ministerial position where she can do little damage. In this cabinet reshuffle, Ramaphosa managed to yield to the internal logic of the ANC, which required that he retain unpopular ministers, while at the same time he listened to the broader society and appointed credible ministers in key government departments. It's a win-win situation. This is what Ramaphosa has to do throughout his leadership whenever key issues are concerned.

If the ANC engages in conflict with the broader society regarding the moral basis of its leadership and justification for its decisions, then Ramaphosa can serve as a mediator by giving each side an opportunity to make its case. This will require that he be seen as a fair arbiter between society and the ANC. He cannot use his position as the president of the country to undermine the ANC as that will have a detrimental impact on his tenure as president of the party. On the other hand, Ramaphosa is expected by the broader society and especially by the private sector to use his position as president of the ANC to manage the party and moderate its distaste for the values held in the broader society.

This points to a type of leadership that is focused on managing crises instead of pursuing a vision. In managing the expectations of the ANC and that of society and allowing for "fair play", Ramaphosa will have to be indecisive on contentious issues, particularly those that pit the ANC against the broader society. It is known that Ramaphosa has taken a cautious position regarding such radical policies as expropriation of land without compensation. In this way he has straddled the middle road and sent out a message that, even while endorsing the EFF's parliamentary motion in this regard, he can be trusted to manage the process and ensure that the ANC does not go overboard in implementing the land policy. This is the leadership style in which indecisiveness appears strategic. The ultimate goal is not to lead the country to the land of milk and honey, but to manage conflict. Perhaps that is what South Africa needs at this stage: a president who acts as referee in an ongoing battle between society and the ANC. In this way, Ramaphosa's main job is to restrain the ANC in its tendency to drift further from society. By allowing him to do this job, the ANC will be rewarded by the votes that Ramaphosa will help the party obtain from the broader society. This does not mean that South Africa will turn the corner on corruption; instead, it means that the country will remain corrupt, but at the same time be functional as a democracy, much like Turkey or Russia.

Leading South Africa in the post-Zuma era is a balancing act which requires the ability to appreciate small gains instead of aiming high and falling hard. In his first act as South Africa's crisis management supremo, Ramaphosa navigated between the wishes of the broader society and the preferences of the ANC on the matter of Zuma's exit from power. I will explain this point further in the next chapter, which focuses on how Ramaphosa has to manage yet another crisis, this one involving the ANC's alliance partners.

4.

Ramaphosa and the
Tripartite Alliance

With Ramaphosa's accession to the leadership of the ANC, it is useful to reflect on the form, relevance and effectiveness of the Tripartite Alliance within the democratic dispensation. Since 1994 individual alliance partners – the ANC, the SACP and COSATU – have each experienced difficulties and challenges to their different roles in a democratic society increasingly characterised by multiple, conflicting interests.

As the senior alliance partner, the ANC has been battling to assert itself as a party capable of managing a complex society. The ANC has been deeply divided, quite often unable to communicate a coherent and compelling vision for the country. The divisions within the ANC have also infiltrated the alliance and affected its partners.

The Communist Party has also had its fair share of problems in a democratic South Africa. It has had to resign itself to playing second fiddle to the governing ANC, in return for having some of its leaders deployed to the ANC-led government. This has made it quite difficult for the SACP to be frank with the ANC when it comes to policies and programmes that the party would like to see implemented. With the deployment of SACP senior leaders to government, the party has tended to be divided and at times mute on contentious policy issues on which they ought to take a firm stance. It has cost the SACP much in terms of credibility to maintain its proximity to the ANC and to government. Who can now forgive the party's uncritical, even misguided support for Jacob Zuma, which was instrumental in securing his accession to the leadership of the ANC at the Polokwane conference in 2007 and his subsequent displacement of Thabo Mbeki as president of the country? Later, the party would even publicly defend Zuma against corruption charges. More recently, the party made a complete about-turn where Zuma was concerned. Thus, when Zuma announced fee-free higher education, the Communist Party took a stand against it, however contradictory to its principles, merely because it was Zuma's doing.

Examples like this are an indication of the sad decline of the intellectual vibrancy and principled integrity of the Communist Party. In their years of solidarity with the ANC against the apartheid regime, the SACP provided deep, often inspiring intellectual reflections on the nature of the struggle. Then, at a critical moment in the negotiations for a transition to democracy, it was the intellectual contribution of Joe Slovo, then general secretary of the party, which provided the critical breakthrough that led to the agreement on a government of national unity.

In comparison, the post-apartheid SACP has been quite mediocre in its contribution to policy development in the country. The party often assumes a yes-or-no response towards the policy positions taken by the ANC. Perhaps what it will be most remembered for is its inadvertent invention of the term "tenderpreneur" to characterise politically connected individuals in the business of acquiring government tenders. In 2011 the party's general secretary, Blade Nzimande, referred in a speech to the danger of "tenderpreneurs" who sought to use the ANC for personal enrichment.[33] In general, one can say that the SACP in the post-apartheid South Africa has not been a source of wisdom for the ANC as an alliance partner. Rather, it has been an additional platform for ANC factional battles.

Turning to COSATU, the trade union federation is the alliance partner that has suffered the most since the beginning of democracy in South Africa. It has had to deal with an increasingly hostile economic environment, which has had a devastating effect on its membership. In 2015, COSATU membership stood at 1.9 million, which meant that "COSATU had [the] same membership as it did 15 years ago [in 1991]".[34] If one takes into consideration especially the retrenchments in the mining sector – where the COSATU-affiliated National Union of Mineworkers (NUM) is no longer the majority union – COSATU has had to contend with adverse

---

33 "Nzimande: Tenderpreneurs trying to steal ANC", *Independent Online*, 18 October 2011. Available at: https://www.iol.co.za/business-report/economy/nzimande-tenderpreneurs-trying-to-steal-anc-1159256 (accessed 13 May 2017).

34 "Cosatu's membership drops", *Jacaranda FM*, 23 November 2015. Available at: https://www.jacarandafm.com/news/news/cosatus-membership-drops/ (accessed 17 May 2017).

economic conditions over which it has had no control. In addition to woes in the mining sector, the manufacturing sector in South Africa has been declining, as elsewhere in the world, because of China's emergence as the world's top exporter of manufactured goods. According to *The Economist,* China is the single biggest beneficiary of globalisation,[35] gobbling up an ever-bigger chunk of the world's manufacturing sector. As a result, for example, the textile industry in South Africa has been decimated by Chinese products flooding the market.[36] COSATU's efforts to lobby for tariffs on Chinese-made products, particularly textiles, have fallen on deaf ears.[37]

Another difficulty that COSATU has had to deal with in post-apartheid South Africa is the decline of its mass appeal and relevance for working people. Despite their deep history of social and political activism and their present material conditions, most South Africans hardly think of themselves as members of a working class in the ideological sense of this concept. What this means is that the existence of a large working class does not guarantee

35 "China has gained hugely from globalisation", *The Economist,* 10 December 2016. Available at: https://www.economist.com/news/china/21711508-so-why-are-its-workers-unhappy-china-has-gained-hugely-globalisation (accessed 3 June 2017).

36 J. Booysen, "Imports killing SA's textile industry", *Independent Online,* 3 July 2015. Available at: https://www.iol.co.za/business-report/economy/imports-killing-sas-textile-industry-1879877 (accessed 4 July 2017).

37 W. Roelf, "Cosatu drops proposed boycott of Springbok gear", *Mail & Guardian,* 13 September 2007. Available at: https://mg.co.za/article/2007-09-13-cosatu-drops-proposed-boycott-of-springbok-gear (accessed 4 July 2017).

that there will be some form of consciousness of being working class. A working class and a class that works are two different things. In South Africa the broader population remains a class that works, and does not necessarily consider itself a working class. For COSATU, this renders leftist-leaning trade unions quite unattractive to the broader society because they tend to be about the working class, and not necessarily about the class that works.

COSATU's legitimacy in post-apartheid South Africa has not held up well. Despite its attempt to cast itself as the representative of the working poor, COSATU is seen, by the mass of unemployed people as well as by others, as the voice of a labour aristocracy who are organised and looked after by their unions at the expense especially of those without work. What is more, the broader South African society has no qualms about the private sector or the capitalist mode of production. Indeed, disturbances of the market system are an unbearable inconvenience that South Africans are never willing to put up with, whatever aims those actions may involve. The EFF has learned this recently to its cost. When the EFF decided to trash stores nationwide of the Swedish retail clothing giant H&M after the company was involved in a racist advertising row,[38] the black middle-class Twitter group, otherwise referred to as "Black Twitter", lambasted the EFF and called on the party to desist from physical harm to property. With no historical animosity towards the market – but only concerned with its unfair distribution of

---

38 "H&M pulls ad after social media outcry over racism", *Eyewitness News*, 8 January 2018. Available at: http://ewn.co.za/2018/01/09/h-and-m-pulls-ad-after-social-media-outcry-over-racism (accessed 8 January 2018).

returns – the growing middle class in South Africa do not make for a good audience for left-leaning unions. Even the poor in South Africa do not frame their concerns as a class matter.

In addition to the difficult conditions in which COSATU has had to survive, the federation also scored some own goals by embroiling itself in unnecessary internal battles. These have seen the departure of the National Union of Metalworkers of South Africa (NUMSA). When NUMSA was expelled from COSATU following differences about the presidency of Zuma, a large part of COSATU's legitimacy left the federation as well. NUMSA, which had fallen out with Zuma over economic and labour policy, accused COSATU of defending his ailing leadership at the expense of pursuing the interests of the workers and the poor. COSATU would ultimately turn hostile towards Zuma,[39] and then give its backing to Cyril Ramaphosa to become president. But COSATU's change of tune did not come about before the federation began bleeding membership.

While alliance members have faced problems in the past two decades of democracy, some of which are problems that would occur in any democratic system, the alliance as a whole has lacked a coordinated response to the challenges that the partners have experienced. The SACP, for one, has been so frustrated with the ANC recently that the party decided to contest local by-elections for the first time in its own right, in effect campaigning against its

---

39   T. Madia and M. Gallens, "Cosatu cancels main Workers' Day rally as Zuma is heckled", *News24*, 1 May 2017. Available at: https://www.news24.com/SouthAfrica/News/cosatu-cancels-main-workers-day-rally-as-zuma-is-heckled-20170501 (accessed 4 May 2017).

alliance partner the ANC.[40] This step seems to have been taken in reaction to a situation where the ANC was no longer paying much attention to the priorities of the alliance and its leaders were becoming more and more embroiled in corruption.

When COSATU and the SACP took the decision to support Cyril Ramaphosa in the ANC's leadership race in 2017,[41] many questions were left unanswered regarding the basic conditions of this support. Except for the historical fact that Ramaphosa helped found NUM and subsequently COSATU, there are currently no obvious reasons why the left-leaning alliance partners should throw their weight behind him. If one considers Ramaphosa's journey and career in the last fifteen years, nothing places him close to COSATU or the Communist Party. Indeed, the SACP's position on what it considers the undue influence of the private sector on the ANC leadership makes Ramaphosa suspect number one. Again, Ramaphosa's controversial relationship with so-called white monopoly capital makes him a natural enemy of a party that has taken a firm line against the domination of monopolies in South Africa's economy.[42] Yet, at the time of the elective conference, it was reported that the SACP "was even considering the formation

---

40 S. Cele and H. Nhlabathi, "Metsimaholo by-elections a test case for SACP", *News24*, 22 October 2017. Available at: https://www.news24.com/SouthAfrica/News/metsimaholo-by-elections-a-test-case-for-sacp-20171021 (accessed 12 November 2017).

41 "Cosatu reiterates support for Ramaphosa to lead ANC", *The Citizen*, 12 July 2017. Available at: https://citizen.co.za/news/south-africa/1570524/cosatu-reiterates-support-ramaphosa-lead-anc/ (accessed 30 July 2017).

42 Z. Ngcobo, "Nzimande: Guptas not the answer to dealing with white monopoly capital", *Eyewitness News*, 10 May 2017. Available at: http://www.sacp.org.za/main.php?ID=6006 (accessed 14 May 2017).

of an 'alternative movement' led by Cyril Ramaphosa if he loses the ANC leadership contest".[43]

By supporting Ramaphosa, it seems the SACP is not denying his association with corporate South Africa, but hopes that Ramaphosa is more benign than the known corporate stooges. Could this be a form of "Stockholm syndrome", whereby captives begin to develop feelings of sympathy for their captors? Is the SACP's inexplicable support of Ramaphosa a survival strategy by a fading organisation?

When pressed to provide the reasons for its support of Rama-phosa during the ANC presidential contest, COSATU insisted that Ramaphosa is not likely to be corrupt because he is already a bil-lionaire in his own right. Gwede Mantashe openly remarked that Ramaphosa is too rich to be tempted to "steal resources".[44] Besides these comments, there are many reasons one can put forth to make the case that Ramaphosa is to be trusted to lead. For one thing, he has come through a complex series of leadership positions in many different sectors and organisations, demonstrating his ability to oper-ate in both the unions and the private sector, for example. This could point to his versatility and capacity to navigate through competing interests. The reasons that were provided by COSATU and the SACP as the basis for their support of Ramaphosa's leadership raise serious concerns as to whether the alliance partners have properly reflected upon this question. Perhaps, after all, the alliance partners were

43   D. Bendile, M. Letsoalo and G. Sigaucwe, "SACP mulls Ramaphosa-led party", *Mail & Guardian*, 14 July 2017. Available at: https://mg.co.za/article/2017-07-14-00-sacp-mulls-ramaphosa-led-party (accessed 30 July 2017).
44   "Ramaphosa is rich, won't be tempted to steal, Mantashe", *eNCA*, 5 January 2018. Available at: https://www.enca.com/south-africa/ramaphosa-is-rich-cant-be-tempted-to-steal-mantashe (accessed 4 February 2018).

looking for any candidate who could save them from the embarrassing Zuma episode in which they failed to exercise caution before betting on the man who turned out to be their worst enemy.

It is also of concern that COSATU and Gwede Mantashe seem to believe that only poor people steal while rich people earn everything fairly. Here is a newsflash: rich people steal through sophisticated schemes. And some smarter rich people normally rig the game in their favour, so that they don't have to go to the trouble of stealing. Ramaphosa deserves more thoughtful and reflective allies than the SACP and COSATU. Their support could in the end amount to a mere rejection of Zuma, and nothing beyond that. If indeed COSATU and the SACP are only concerned about putting Zuma behind them, with their support of Ramaphosa as an avenue to express that, then the friendship that has been struck between the SACP, COSATU and Ramaphosa will not withstand the test of time.

Anti-corruption is not enough to sustain the relationship between Ramaphosa and the alliance partners. Indeed, although Ramaphosa's measured anti-corruption stance turned them in his direction as they fled the gathering storm around Zuma and his nosediving popularity, there ought to be more to this new relationship. For the relationship to blossom and deliver stability within the alliance, it is necessary that the alliance partners discuss the basic conditions for the "new dawn"[45] that Ramaphosa claims his

---

45   W. Roelf, "South Africa's Ramaphosa hails 'new dawn', warns of tough decisions", *Reuters*, 16 February 2018. Available at: https://www.reuters.com/article/us-safrica-politics/south-africas-ramaphosa-hails-new-dawn-warns-of-tough-decisions-idUSKCN1G00PV (accessed 16 February 2018).

accession to power heralds for the ANC and for the country. For there are wide differences of opinion between the alliance partners that need to be discussed. When it comes to policy matters, for instance, the SACP could not be further from Ramaphosa's market-friendly solutions to the ills of society. As a member of the National Planning Commission, Ramaphosa was part of the team that drafted the National Development Plan (NDP), and in his maiden State of the Nation address, he pledged to implement the NDP as a vehicle of economic growth.[46] Yet the same plan has been rejected as a "neoliberal framework"[47] by the SACP.

While COSATU after its years of battering may be glad to be associated with Ramaphosa's "new dawn", some unions with a history of being associated with progressive politics in the country have rather taken a cautious approach towards his presidency. The militant NUMSA criticised COSATU for its endorsement of Ramaphosa, arguing that his administration would be no different from Zuma's when it came to matters of corruption.[48] For NUMSA, Ramaphosa's leadership means a new war against workers, for it

---

46   T. Sithole, "Ramaphosa: My new deal for SA – and 10-point action plan for jobs, growth, transformation", *BizNews*, 14 November 2017. Available at: https://www.biznews.com/thought-leaders/2017/11/14/ramaphosa-new-deal-for-sa/ (accessed 16 November 2017).

47   SACP, "Let's not monumentalize the National Development Plan", 14 May 2013. Available at: http://www.sacp.org.za/main.php?ID=3972 (accessed 16 November 2017).

48   M. Gallens, "Ramaphosa presidency would be no different to Zuma", *News24*, 25 November 2016. Available at: https://www.news24.com/SouthAfrica/News/ramaphosa-presidency-would-be-no-different-to-zuma-numsa-20161125 (accessed 3 October 2017).

is suspected that he harbours an ideological position against the workers, which some say found expression in the Marikana massacre. Will Ramaphosa's leadership amount to a mere "facelift" for the ANC, as NUMSA would say? Or does it provide a fresh opportunity for rethinking a broader social accord involving government, business, labour and civil society? Ramaphosa emphasised in his maiden State of the Nation address that he aims to build a "broad compact on infrastructure with business and organised labour".[49] While this does not amount to much when it comes to specific areas of compromise between business and labour, the message is that there is a need for those key stakeholders to return to the table and resume talks on major issues.

As much as there are problems within the alliance, particularly in relation to labour, there are even bigger problems with unions outside the alliance. These have been steadily gaining ground as meaningful representatives of workers in the country. One notable example is the Association of Mineworkers and Construction Union (AMCU), which has challenged the dominance of the COSATU-aligned NUM especially in the platinum mining sector. Over time NUM's proximity to the ruling ANC eroded its legitimacy as representative of workers and created a space for a more militant approach in the mining labour sector. It was the Marikana massacre of August 2012 that afforded AMCU the opportunity to unseat the once unassailable NUM from its former dominant position in the platinum sector. AMCU used the

---

49   Government Communication and Information System, "State of the Nation address", 16 February 2018.

Marikana shooting to point to what happens to workers when the ANC elite, corporate South Africa and unions such as NUM collaborate behind a political agenda.

The other unions that Ramaphosa will have to watch carefully are the public sector unions, which often take a militant attitude towards government whenever the interests of their members are affected.

After NUMSA's expulsion from COSATU in 2014, COSATU came to be dominated by public sector unions. The domination of public sector unions means that COSATU might have to tone down its militancy, since it no longer represents poor workers. ANC national chairperson Gwede Mantashe, an experienced trade unionist, warned COSATU that its reliance on public sector unions spells trouble for the worker consciousness within the federation. The public sector unions within COSATU, however, always take a militant stance towards government as an employer, so the jury is out on this issue.

In his first State of the Nation address, Ramaphosa hinted that he would consider downsizing the bloated public service in the interest of efficiency and economy. It will indeed be interesting to see if Ramaphosa can manage to shed jobs in government, as this would bring him into direct confrontation with militant unions such as the South African Democratic Teachers Union (SADTU) and the National Health, Education and Allied Workers' Union (NEHAWU). This is a no-go area for him, especially with the general elections looming in 2019. And should he try to resort to using outside consultants as a way of resolving the problems of an overstaffed and inefficient public service, he will also come in for criticism from the unions. Moreover, in this event the EFF is unlikely to avoid the opportunity to step into the fray and extract some political mileage from it, accusing Ramaphosa of pursuing a neoliberal agenda. This critique will further cement the view that Ramaphosa is only interested in protecting his friends in the private sector.

So far, however, Ramaphosa has been able to promise everything to everyone. In his State of the Nation address, he promised austerity measures to cut frills in government; vowed to take a strong stand against corruption; and undertook to find money to fund some of the radical economic policies adopted at the Nasrec conference, including free tertiary education, the policy that Zuma dropped in the ANC's lap as his parting gift. The subsequent budget, which was tabled in Parliament on 16 February 2018, spoke a different language, however, and it showed that Ramaphosa cannot possibly satisfy everyone, particularly his alliance partners. The decision to increase value-added tax (VAT), as announced in the budget, has demonstrated that Ramaphosa's friendship with COSATU and the SACP may be severely tested. In responding to the VAT hike, the SACP stated that Ramaphosa was overburdening the poor while letting the rich carry on with their lives of opulence. COSATU also expressed its "disappointment" at Ramaphosa's budget, which it said overburdened the workers. In fact, it seems from the expression of opinion within various sections of the ANC (such as the ANC Gauteng branch) that the president's decision to increase VAT may not have been the subject of full consultation with the alliance and within the broad ANC.

What is the moral basis for increasing VAT compared to a targeted tax such as corporate tax? As far as the SACP and COSATU are concerned, a targeted tax is not only a method to increase revenue for government, but it is also about pursuing social justice. In most countries, including Western democracies, an increase in corporate tax is the best way to get something from companies in return for society bearing the burden of some of the costs from the operation of the business sector. Business externalises many of its costs to the broader society, while internalising returns. Therefore, the best way the society can be reimbursed is to extract value by way of corporate tax. In this respect the first budget of the Ramaphosa presidency shows a lack of perspective, and this spells trouble for his relationship with the trade unions.

All the same, in Ramaphosa the alliance partners COSATU and the SACP may have stumbled upon someone they can work with. There are indeed serious policy differences between Ramaphosa and the alliance partners that require a deeper conversation. Ramaphosa may be good for the SACP and COSATU, but they are yet to explain how they arrived at the decision to support him. If this question is not faced, the alliance will continue to limp from one crisis to another. For someone who needs solid friends to sustain his presidency, Ramaphosa needs to look further than the alliance partners.

5.

Friends and Foes

— ∿∿ —

No matter who you are or what your credentials, it is no easy task to lead South Africa. With its diversity of people and problems, there are many challenges and pitfalls. This is something the newly elected president, Cyril Ramaphosa, already knows. During his first few weeks in office it was already clear that his term as president would be no picnic. What will it take for him to survive and succeed in this very challenging role? And who does he have on his side to help him succeed?

A quick glance at world history and current world politics shows that humankind has had more extensive experience with leadership failure than with leadership success. In all the various fields of human endeavour, whether politics, the military, business and so on, it is difficult to find great numbers of really successful leaders. Then, too, there are more successful leaders than respectable ones.

One example of this close to home is Jacob Zuma, whose leadership style can be characterised as "Machiavellian" because of his uncanny ability to survive against all the odds. In this sense he certainly was successful.

Another thing about Zuma was that he selected his friends very carefully, not because of their wisdom or moral stature, but solely on the basis of their ability to provide him with the means of survival. In the end, he left office not really because he was brought down but because his term as the ANC president had come to an end.

Only time will tell whether Ramaphosa has the same ability to survive the many political storms and challenges he faces. To better understand what it will take for Ramaphosa to survive, we need first of all to look at how he came to power. In the first place it needs to be said that Ramaphosa was not elected the president of the ANC because his integrity agenda had won the hearts and minds of the party branch delegations who voted at Nasrec in December 2017. He came to power, not with the help of friends and allies, but on the back of a strange conglomeration of interest groups and stakeholders who invested in his bid for office. This unfortunate situation will have a defining impact on his leadership of the country.

The ANC went into Nasrec consisting of two main factions, replicated perfectly in the broader society outside the party. The first was aligned to Zuma and it sought to challenge the domination of the market in policy formulation in the country. This faction backed Nkosazana Dlamini-Zuma and conveniently packaged her candidature as a quest for the self-determination of black people, or, more crudely, "leave us alone to be as corrupt as we want with our own African resources". This idea had some traction in the broader society. On the other side was the anti-Zuma faction, which was appropriated by Ramaphosa, a candidate who campaigned on an integrity ticket. Ramaphosa was also aligned with some key figures in the private sector, who believed that his ability to tell inflation from stagnation made him a safe bet for their interests.

In the end, neither of these factions won at Nasrec. Although Ramaphosa secured the presidency, the other preferred candidates on his slate were left in the cold, apart from a latecomer to Ramaphosa's corner, Gwede Mantashe. Mantashe has been the ANC's secretary general throughout Zuma's disastrous two terms at the helm of the organisation. During those years, Mantashe was Zuma's fixer, quelling any possible revolt against Zuma in the party. As Zuma's term as president of the ANC wound down in 2016 and 2017, Mantashe strategically began to gradually distance himself from Zuma, and started to offer veiled support to Ramaphosa as an alternative. His knowledge of the internal machinery of the party must have made him an attractive addition to Ramaphosa, who needed a party hack like Mantashe to help him manage the ANC.

When he entered the race to lead the ANC, Ramaphosa may have believed that if he won he could install his entire slate in the top six positions in the ANC and, thus equipped and armed, could speedily proceed to implement his agenda. As mentioned earlier, what came out of the Nasrec conference, however, was not what Ramaphosa had bargained for. He was instead confronted with a many-headed monster, which had been put in place by the so-called

Premier League – comprising former Mpumalanga premier David Mabuza, former Free State premier Ace Magashule and former North West premier Supra Mahumapelo. What they effected at Nasrec was a great betrayal. This group was formerly aligned to President Zuma and they were believed to support Dlamini-Zuma's candidature. But at Nasrec they made a cold, calculated move which saw them betraying Zuma and installing Ramaphosa as president. This was dishonest, even by Zuma's own standards. Both Magashule and Mabuza landed into the ANC's top six, the latter emerging as vice president. It was the stuff one expects to see only in a high-end Hollywood drama based on political machinations in Washington, DC.

If there is anything the Premier League knows, it is how to run up political victories and win leadership contests. Even before the Nasrec elective conference, the trio had apparently been laying the deck. They began their work at the Congress of South African Students (COSAS) conference, which would elect young and talented Zuma stooges. From there they went on to engineer the results of the ANC Youth League elections, which saw a Zuma defender in the form of Collen Maine taking over in 2015. Thereafter they secured Bathabile Dlamini as head of the ANC Women's League, another Zuma defender and a disaster in her own right. All this was an object lesson in how to put together a complex league of allies to sway the all-important ANC elective conference, winning it without even contesting it.

In the period leading up to Nasrec, I was convinced that it was going to be Mabuza's conference. Mabuza used his power base to ensure that neither of the two factions that contested the elections could claim victory and that he and the Premier League could play a determining role in securing the outcomes they wanted. Ramaphosa must surely be aware that he owes it to the Premier League for rescuing his ailing candidature and saving it from a non-performing faction.

What is even more serious, Ramaphosa will need the support of the Premier League in order to survive as leader of the ANC. Mabuza, Ramaphosa's deputy, has already offered his friendship to Ramaphosa, having needlessly stated to the public that he will "protect"[50] Ramaphosa. Mabuza knows full well that Ramaphosa finds himself far from friends following the Nasrec conference. Indeed, Ramaphosa ought to be frantically recruiting friends since he left a number of them behind when he made it to the head of the ANC.

What does one make of a leader who has been elected under such circumstances? If one ascends to power in this way, one knows for sure one was not brought there by one's own fortune, but by the fortune of others. This means that in one way or another, Ramaphosa will soon have to begin to service his debt and pay back those who invested in him. It is inevitable that not all of those who invested will receive returns or enjoy equal returns on equity. This will have political consequences. Those who feel that they are not receiving their due may be inclined to disinvest, either by turning on him or by looking for someone else to advance their interests. Can Ramaphosa avoid being too beholden to those who brought

---

50 T. Madia, "I will protect the ANC president: David Mabuza", *News24*, 28 January 2018. Available at: https://www.news24.com/SouthAfrica/News/i-will-protect-the-anc-president-david-mabuza-20180128 (accessed 31 January 2018).

him to power and remain his own man, making his own decisions about the direction in which the country ought to move? It is much easier to win a leadership battle than to stay a leader once victory has been achieved.

As a leader who did not rise to power because his own political agenda was approved, Ramaphosa should focus on rebuilding his own base and redefining his leadership. He cannot do that without risking alienating those who actually helped him. While the help of the Premier League in his accession to power is clear, we should not discount the role of the private sector. For it was the private sector's endorsement of Ramaphosa as a desirable candidate and personification of political good sense, and the legitimacy that came with this, that made Ramaphosa an attractive commodity for the Premier League. While Zuma's supporters cried conspiracy when corporate South Africa came out in Ramaphosa's support, members of the Premier League knew that Zuma's preferred candidate, Dlamini-Zuma, was a hard sell whichever way one viewed it. The Premier League were no swans themselves; many of them have serious allegations of corruption and even worse hanging above their heads. Magashule is facing a probe into his alleged role in the Vrede dairy farm project, from which the Gupta family benefited enormously. Mabuza cannot shake the image of a provincial power baron who has been accused of ordering the assassination of political rivals and corruption-busting comrades – whether such an allegation is true or not. For a trio that desperately needs credibility, Ramaphosa seemed an attractive option. Standing in his company and serving him would help to rehabilitate their negative public images – in Mabuza's case, perhaps in preparation for his own presidency one day. And in return Ramaphosa would gain a half-victory – still better than none at all.

To my mind, the most powerful interest groups that President Ramaphosa should worry about are the Premier League and corporate South Africa. Neither of the two groups would count as historical friends of Ramaphosa, although the private sector did provide Ramaphosa with asylum when he left politics at the end of Mandela's presidency. In the tussle for domination that will grow between these two interest groups, a few crumbs may fall to the ground from the bread fought over. The mass of South Africans may have to pick them up in order to survive the day. To make sure this is not what awaits us, Ramaphosa must avoid the extreme demands of these two groups, and forge his own agenda based on the interests of the broader population. In that way, Ramaphosa will be undertaking the difficult but doable task of building a better foundation for the new country.

No doubt Ramaphosa has more than enough enemies. But who are Ramaphosa's friends? He has had many different types of friends over the years since showing an interest in public life. He has been involved, successively, in the student movement, in the trade union movement, in the Mass Democratic Movement, in constitutional negotiations, in the business sector and, latterly, in politics. He has adapted to difficult situations and uncomfortable company, including having to serve alongside Zuma as his deputy while knowing that Zuma and his allies were all along plotting his political demise. Although this shows adaptability, it also leaves unanswered the question: what are the core principles of such a leader?

One of the things that will be missed about Zuma is the

simplicity of his thinking. Zuma never had to deal with mixed agendas. He only kept the company of people who were stealing with him and keeping him out of prison. With Ramaphosa the picture is different: there are too many conflicting agendas circulating around him and seeking his attention, claiming to represent the interests of the broader society. He seems to be trying to please everyone. Furthermore, there are too many people and groups that consider him their friends. He needs to tread carefully with all of them. For one thing, he needs to shun the flattery of the corporate sector, who believe their champion has won the race to lead the ANC, and at the same time make it clear to them that he cannot renege on the radical policy resolutions adopted by the ANC at Nasrec, including the expropriation of land without compensation. One way or another, Ramaphosa will have to persuade corporate South Africa to allow him to build the foundations for a power base for himself within the ANC. The best thing the private sector can do to assist Ramaphosa in this regard is to desist from constantly flattering him and setting unrealistic targets for him.

As for the Premier League, Ramaphosa faces several challenges here. One is that the trio might use the Zuma faction, to which they were first attached, to threaten his stability if he does not play ball with them. However, in my view, Ramaphosa is in a good position to forge his own agenda amid the conflicting interests that emerged at Nasrec. He will have to navigate between the competing agendas and interests of the people who surround him within the ANC and outside the party. He also has to do certain things for the broader South African population, especially the poor, whose views are not necessarily reflected in the agendas pushed by different interest groups. Ramaphosa has enough good friends, people who are on his side. The best friendship he can build and rely upon is the one involving the broader South African population. He has to learn to speak to them using a completely different language from the one he uses when conversing with his political allies. Ramaphosa cannot build this new friendship without shaking the foundations of the current relations he has with various groups, factions and lobbies within and outside the ANC. This is a risky undertaking, but it has a potential to shape his presidency.

6.

Ramaphosa's Hill

———·⁓·———

I have often been struck by the significance of hills and mountains in battles, both military and political. History is full of accounts of notable and decisive combats that were fought on this form of topography. Here at home, the hill of Isandhlwana in Zululand comes to mind as the place where a Zulu army overran one of the world's mightiest military machines of the nineteenth century, killing some thirteen hundred soldiers fighting on the British side, including 779 British soldiers.[51] Turning further afield and striking a more political key, one can think of Capitol Hill in Washington, DC, where the US Congress is located. Americans often refer to it simply

---

51 South African History Online, "Zulu army defeat British army at the Isandlwana mountain", 19 January 2012. Available at: http://www.sahistory.org.za/ dated-event/zulu-army-defeat-british-army-isandlwana-mountain (accessed 15 January 2018).

as "the Hill", which somehow conveys the sense of a topography where decisive battles in the country are fought between the executive and the legislature. This is where the power and skill of any American president is tested. Donald Trump's disastrous first year as the 45th president of the United States has shown how the powerful lawmakers on the Hill can scupper any presidential policy they are not happy with, even if it might be in the interests of the people. Trump has thus far been unable to seize the Hill, and his Twitter feed consists of daily instalments from an ever-frustrated president who can't win control or obtain the cooperation and support he needs for the success of his agenda. It is reported that as a result Trump surrenders to comfort eating, gobbling nachos and washing them down with fizzy drinks throughout the day.

Each and every leader has his or her hill to climb – the troubles that they cannot wish away in the course of their leadership. Besides the internal problems he will encounter from his colleagues in the ANC, Cyril Ramaphosa has inherited a political system that favours court litigation against the government of the day, which usually ends up at Constitution Hill in Johannesburg. This is where South Africa's Constitutional Court sits, a place of historical importance because of its association with the anti-apartheid movement in the country. Constitution Hill used to be a jail where prominent anti-apartheid activists were incarcerated.[52] The Hill, as I shall refer to Constitution Hill, is already becoming a key policy battleground, akin to Capitol Hill in the American political system. This is because the South African Constitution allows for the laws

---

52   https://www.constitutionhill.org.za/sites/site-womens-jail (accessed 31 January 2018).

of Parliament and for policy implementation to be subjected to judicial review to ensure that they do not conflict with the provisions and principles of the Constitution and the Bill of Rights. The practice of judicial review is one of the aspects of the political system that warrant a comparison between Constitution Hill and Capitol Hill. Both hills reflect the state and level of political development and engagement in their respective countries.

Some of the interventions that the Constitutional Court has undertaken in recent years may have been triggered by the ailing state of Parliament, which continually failed to rein in former president Zuma's rogue executive. Instead of exercising its constitutional responsibility to hold government to account, Parliament became a surrogate of the executive, with the opposition parties mounting hopeless resistance against the compliance and deference of the ANC majority. The ANC caucus in Parliament became extremely partisan, consequently abdicating the oversight function of Parliament to the courts. The courts in turn welcomed this "new" responsibility, openly questioning the soundness of some of the policy decisions made by the ANC, while maintaining that there was no judicial overreach involved, as the ANC often claimed in reaction.

The ANC government's blunders and its failure to adhere to good governance in policy implementation created a situation where the courts had to babysit the executive. A classic example of this was the Constitutional Court's attempt to resolve the social grant payment crisis that had developed under the Department of Social Development. What it did was to nullify the contract that the South African Social Security Agency (SASSA) had entered into with the controversial, politically connected service provider Cash Paymaster Services (CPS).[53] When SASSA ignored a judgment by the court that a new service provider should be appointed once the illegally constituted agreement with CPS came to an end, the court involved itself in monitoring the department's compliance with the judgment. This meant that the court had to evaluate each and every step that the department took in implementing the judgment. The department was then placed under a form of curatorship, where it had to report to the court on its progress. This experience shows how policy implementation could be carried out through Constitution Hill, as opposed to the Union Buildings. So far, there has not been an indication of judicial restraint by the Constitutional Court, perhaps rightfully so. This is because in most of the cases, it was clear to the general public that government was in the wrong even before the courts said so.

Policy battles have become quite intense in South African politics, to a point where they involve tactics similar to those of military battles. Such policy battles take place both within the ANC among comrades and between the ANC and the opposition parties. The big policy squabbles in South Africa began to emerge under Jacob Zuma's tenure as president of the party when the ANC began to evaluate its broader policy framework. At its national policy conference held at Gallagher Estate in 2012, the party sought to find a "vision for a second transition that must focus on the social and

---

53   E. Evans, "Hulley had 'no role' in R10bn Sassa social grant tender", *Mail & Guardian*, 11 September 2013. Available at: https://mg.co.za/article/2013-09-11-hulley-had-no-role-in-r10bn-sassa-social-grant-tender (accessed 15 July 2017).

economic transformation of South Africa in the next 30 to 50 years". It introduced the theme of "The second transition? Building a national democratic society".[54] Since the ANC laid bare its frustration with the slow pace of social and economic change in the country, the party has not advanced much further in finding ways to achieve its long-term transformational goals.

While the ANC was busy searching for appropriate visions, internal divisions within the party escalated from the state of petty squabbles and hardened into ideological positions. The ANC membership became divided between those who favoured radical economic policy directions and those who believed in a moderate approach. These divisions were also present at the Nasrec conference in 2017. There is little doubt that major policy battles are set to take place in the coming years and many will be fought out on Constitution Hill.

Although in the last decade most judgments at the Hill came in the form of evaluations of former president Zuma's controversial decisions or those of his ministers, the end of Zuma's tenure will not bring an end to the involvement of the Constitutional Court in the political process. If a case is winnable and has political implications, there will always be someone willing to take it to the Hill. Although the ANC may no longer be required to support legal battles with personal implications, such as those fought by Zuma to ensure his political survival, the reality is that the ANC will be

---

54   ANC, "The second transition? Building a national democratic society and the balance of forces in 2012: A discussion document towards the National Policy Conference", 27 February 2012. Available at: http://www.anc.org.za/docs/discus/2012/transition.pdf (accessed 20 January 2018).

forced to engage with its opponents in the forum of the Constitutional Court, irrespective of what it feels about the use of the courts in dealing with policy contests.

It has been clear thus far that the ANC government, particularly during the Zuma years, has consistently shifted away from consensus politics in favour of majoritarianism. The essence of multiparty democracy is that all political parties represented in Parliament should make a contribution when it comes to making laws. The Founding Provisions of the Constitution of South Africa state explicitly that ours "is a multiparty system of democratic government".[55] Such a system favours a consensus approach towards policy formulation and implementation. This is not to say that the will of the majority will no longer prevail. It means, instead, that the majority shall not arbitrarily impose its will on minorities. Democracy is more than a mere expression of majority will. Democracy is also sometimes about restraining the majority, at times for their own good.

South Africa's experience with democracy under Zuma's tenure is a clear indication that majority decisions are not always the most rational or beneficial. Under Zuma, Parliament made decisions that could be seen as legitimate from the point of view that they were approved by the majority. However, some of those decisions that passed through majority processes have proved to be irrational, indefensible and even unconstitutional.

An interesting example of the danger of an unrestrained majority for democratic processes can be seen in how Parliament dealt

---

55   The Constitution of the Republic of South Africa, Act 108 of 1996.

with the Public Protector's report on the upgrades to Zuma's private residence at Nkandla. The ANC used its majority in Parliament to absolve Zuma from taking responsibility and paying back a certain portion of the public money spent on his private residence. Opposition parties wanted Zuma to be held liable and insisted that the ANC was abusing its majority on the matter. The Constitutional Court subsequently ruled that Zuma had failed to protect the Constitution and that he should pay back some of the money spent on Nkandla, as the Public Protector recommended. Had Parliament adopted a multiparty stance with all represented political parties engaging fairly together on how to deal with and give effect to the recommendations of the Nkandla report, sanity might have prevailed and the matter might not have had to be forwarded to the court for arbitration. In general, the relations between the majority political party and the opposition parties in South Africa are tense and very combative. The manner in which the parties engage with each other on issues like the Public Protector's report shows lack of commitment to the principle of a multiparty system, or at least the spirit of multiparty democracy.

The opposition parties are battle-hardened to the point where they are willing to go to court and challenge many of the decisions that the ANC-led government has arrived at on the strength of its majority vote. The ANC, on the other hand, is not willing to negotiate on such matters, often flaunting its electoral and parliamentary majority as the main justification for its policy decisions. In all fairness, a decision should not be justified only on the basis of how it was arrived at. Decisions should also make sense in the broader context within society. This is what legal scholars refer to as a "culture of justification", which ought to set democratic South Africa apart from apartheid South Africa. Apartheid South Africa did not operate in a manner in which it justified its decisions, especially not to the majority of citizens, who were excluded from playing a role in the decision-making process. The experience of democracy in the last decade shows that a majority position can be abused not only in respect of minorities, but it can also be manipulated against public interests.

When a court is asked to step in to evaluate some of the decisions arrived at through a majority showing, the court's role is to ensure that the public interest is secured. At times the public interest can contradict the will of the majority, and vice versa. The idea of judicial review – the principle that allows a court to evaluate the conduct of all organs of state including government – is there to ensure that the majority does not unduly impose its will on the minority. In reality, this means that the court can at times assume an activist role to protect the political minority. Yet, as experience has shown, whenever the courts in South Africa embark on activism to protect political minorities, they are accused by the ANC of allowing themselves to be used for political gain. This criticism shows that the principle of judicial review is an irritant to the ANC.

Events in South Africa over the last decade should teach us that justifying a decision solely on the basis that it is favoured by the majority is an approach that should be permanently viewed with suspicion. It can be argued that the greatest threat to democracy is not only its vulnerability to takeover by elites, but also the tyranny of the majority. In his celebrated work on political philosophy,

Friedrich Hayek saw the tyranny of the majority as "the road to serfdom".[56]

If we believe that sometimes it is in the public interest to restrain the majority, then we should appreciate the role of the courts in drawing that line whenever we feel a government policy or decision is unclear or at fault. The Constitutional Court in South Africa has a key role to play in giving practical meaning to the Constitution. In discharging its constitutional obligation, the court is also making itself available as a forum for major policy battles in the country. This phenomenon of policy battles being referred to Constitution Hill will not come to an end anytime soon. As various interest groups define and form themselves amid the evolution of the political life of the country, the battles at the Hill will only intensify, reflecting the constant shifts and developments in society. The Constitutional Court is a theatre of choice when it comes to major policy contests in the country.

Indeed, there are civil society organisations that have been formed with the sole purpose of litigating on policy with the aim of undoing what they consider to be unjust and unreasonable decisions by government. Going to court tends to produce quick results for the litigants, and it provides good political mileage as well as conferring legitimacy. The Afrikaner lobby group AfriForum has been at the forefront of the process of approaching the Hill to fight policy battles. Some of the issues that AfriForum has taken on review include affirmative action and school admission policies. These represent just a few of the issues that will be fought over in

---

56   F. Hayek, *The Road to Serfdom*. London: Routledge, 1994.

the Constitutional Court in the coming years. The exercise of executive power will remain a permanent point of contest at the Hill.

There is nothing fundamentally wrong with the principle of judicial review, the testing of the exercise of power in the courts. The problem is that court litigation on policy is no substitute for the political process. The courts are inherently incapable of resolving political problems. With an increasing number of political squabbles being referred to the Hill, it is important for South Africans to ask whether this phenomenon does not unduly overburden the courts, whose jurisprudence is still in the making. Will the Constitutional Court cope with the intensity of the battles it is expected to host in the coming years? These will include such major issues as expropriation of land without compensation, on which Parliament has recently passed a motion, thus paving the way for one of the fiercest constitutional battles ever,[57] as it sets government policy on a collision course with the Bill of Rights. The implementation of radical economic policies will spark even more court litigation.

But perhaps a recent intervention by Ramaphosa in the matter of the mining charter produced by the Department of Minerals and Energy may indicate a new approach by his government. Even though the Chamber of Mines had approached the High Court to challenge some of the charter's radical clauses,[58] Ramaphosa intervened in the first few weeks of his presidency by asking the parties to hold back from the court process and allow for further

---

57   R. Pather, "First step to land expropriation without compensation", *Mail & Guardian*, 27 February 2018.

58   A. Seccombe, "Ownership levels of miners put to the test", *Business Day*, 10 November 2017.

consultations on the matter. The parties agreed. While it is too early to make definite conclusions or predictions, this interesting step does seem to indicate that Ramaphosa wants to avoid the bruising battles that his party has fought, and often lost, at the Hill. This will have implications too for the kind of democracy we have in South Africa.

7.

Can Ramaphosa's ANC Win 2019?

———~~~———

Will the ANC manage to secure an absolute majority in the 2019 national and provincial elections or will the party's support fall below 50% for the first time in South Africa's democratic history? And how does the Cyril Ramaphosa card influence the ANC's chances? My basic observation is that the ANC is on a rescue mission and the party's approach to the 2019 elections should be understood as such – a recovery effort. There is a definite time frame for this recovery mission. It started when Ramaphosa was elected the president of the party and it should start to bear fruit by the time the elections are held in 2019, possibly after June in that year. Throughout this ANC's recovery journey, the opposition parties will have minimum effect on how this story is told. The story of electoral politics in post-apartheid South Africa comes down to whether the ANC wins or loses elections. In fact, the opposition parties seem to have resigned themselves to picking up the losses of the ANC, instead of orchestrating such losses. The 2019 elections therefore are about whether or not the ANC will stage a successful recovery from the past decade of degeneration, corruption and lethargy within government. It is not about whether the party will implement innovative policies or deal with the huge challenges of poverty and unemployment facing the country.

For the ANC, the road to the 2019 elections has presented itself in the form of two options. One option was the continuation of Jacob Zuma's legacy, in one form or another. This would have entailed the election of Nkosazana Dlamini-Zuma to succeed Zuma as president of the ANC. Had she won the battle, her victory would have been interpreted as the triumph of the corruption enterprise at the centre of South Africa's politics. Cast as someone who was flanked by compromised and corrupt individuals, including alleged criminal gangs,[59] Dlamini-Zuma's leadership accession would have presented an immediate uphill battle for the ANC going into the 2019 elections. During the contest Dlamini-Zuma did not put much effort into repelling the idea that her victory would amount to an obituary for the ANC in the forthcoming elections. Her attitude was to soldier through, despite a hostile public mood that was gathering around her.

Moreover, Dlamini-Zuma did not come out well in the media, and she appeared to be lost in the maze of a growing public per-

---

59 M. wa Afrika, "Smoked out! NDZ hanging out with cigarette smuggler and gambling tycoon", *Sunday Times*, 15 November 2017. Available at: https://www.timeslive.co.za/sunday-times/news/2017-11-04-smoked-out-ndz-hanging-out-with-cigarette-smuggler-and-gambling-tycoon/ (accessed 25 November 2017).

ception that she was merely a "mini-Zuma". In a television gaffe, the SABC's 24-hour TV news channel erroneously displayed the caption "Mini-Zuma"[60] during a video of Dlamini-Zuma talking about her campaign. Whether that was an innocent mistake by an overworked SABC production team or a deliberate act of sabotage by a disgruntled SABC employee does not matter. The message that came across quite clearly was that Dlamini-Zuma could not shake off the credibility problems that came with the Zuma name. She was not seen as a leader in her own right. Indeed, she was already characterised as an electoral liability for the party in 2019.[61]

On the other side of the contest was the Ramaphosa project, an opportunity for the ANC to return to its glory days. At the same time as running for the presidency of the ANC, Ramaphosa also pursued a parallel campaign through which he positioned himself as the most reasonable choice both for the ANC and for the country. During the contest, his campaign to lead the ANC was already viewed as a threat to the opposition parties in the 2019 elections. Ramaphosa seemed to be the worst thing that could happen to the opposition parties after thriving under Zuma's tenure.[62]

60 "SABC declares Dlamini-Zuma 'Mini-Zuma'", *The Citizen*, 7 August 2017. Available at: https://citizen.co.za/news/news-eish/1602470/sabc-declares-dlamini-zuma-mini-zuma/ (accessed 2 September 2017).

61 T. Madia, "Dlamini-Zuma won't help ANC in 2019", *News24*, 25 August 2016. Available at: https://www.news24.com/SouthAfrica/News/dlamini-zuma-wont-help-anc-in-2019-20160825 (accessed 2 September 2017).

62 "A win for Ramaphosa could cost the DA: Poll", *Business Tech*, 12 December 2017. Available at: https://businesstech.co.za/news/government/216041/a-win-for-ramaphosa-could-cost-the-da-poll/ (accessed 21 December 2017).

What was also quite distinct about Ramaphosa's campaign was its strong element of appeal to those outside the ANC, in that it tried to position him as a credible leader both within and outside the party. Within the ANC, however, Ramaphosa's campaign was viewed with suspicion mainly because it was crafted to appeal as well to those outside, those who did not even participate in the process of voting for ANC president. I myself had concerns with Ramaphosa's campaign within the party, in the sense that it was branded outside the ANC and had more traction outside the party than within. It is common for ANC members to move away from someone who enjoys support from outside the party. For ANC members, being preferred by those outside the party – particularly the private sector and some civil society organisations – is seen as an indication that the ANC agenda might be at risk in the hands of such a leader. During Ramaphosa's campaign a website was created for him, with ANC colours, and yet it was more about the personal branding of Ramaphosa as an alternative to Dlamini-Zuma and the entire Zuma clan. Never before had an ANC presidential candidate crafted a campaign that relied so heavily on external approval as a basis for attracting ANC members to give him their vote.

Ramaphosa also made himself readily available to the media, and he used the media to drive his ideas about where he wanted to take the ANC, in a way that has not been seen in recent times in the party. He used the media to his advantage, and he engaged fully with journalists. If Zuma was gifted in ignoring the reality around him, Ramaphosa is gifted in coming across as capable of saying all things to all men at the same time. While Dlamini-Zuma shunned the media and lacked a strategy on how to respond to some of the negative stories published about her relationship with the controversial Gupta family, Ramaphosa was solicitous about media attention.

When, for example, I wrote a column in which I argued that Ramaphosa's campaign was too weak to dislodge Zuma on its own,[63] a senior member of Ramaphosa's team reached out to me and indicated that my conclusion was too hasty and I should give them a chance to spell out what they were planning to do. As an analyst and not a lobbyist, I indicated that what mattered was not whether I personally understood where Ramaphosa's campaign was headed, but rather how it appeared in the eyes of ordinary ANC branch members. I said that the campaign was much too visible outside the ANC while appearing to be subdued within the party. I also remarked that I was struck by how Ramaphosa's campaign seemed to pay attention to opinion makers and journalists' views of him, instead of focusing on where it mattered: within the ANC. All in all, Ramaphosa's efforts to explain his campaign even to those who did not vote in the ANC elective conference show how the broader population outside the ANC came close to influencing the election outcome.

Had Dlamini-Zuma won the ANC presidency, she would have had to put together a new team to repair her image as she took the party to the 2019 elections. With Ramaphosa, however, his

---

63   R. Mathekga, "Ramaphosa's campaign is doomed", *News24*, 17 April 2017. Available at: https://www.news24.com/Columnists/Ralph_Mathekga/ramaphosas-campaign-is-doomed-20170417 (accessed 5 May 2017).

externally focused campaign to lead the ANC in 2017 was already making good progress in presenting him to the outside world as a leader of the country. Unlike Dlamini-Zuma, Ramaphosa did not have to deal with the narrative that his victory might result in the party struggling to attain the majority required to form a government after the 2019 elections. The reality is that the ANC was given the option either to elect Dlamini-Zuma and suffer defeat in 2019 or to elect Ramaphosa and be given an opportunity to recover. Merely by electing Ramaphosa in 2017, the party has earned an opportunity to recover. Thus, Ramaphosa himself does not have to earn that opportunity further by demonstrating any really substantive success.

There is no need to ask what type of vision South Africa wishes to aspire to as the country shifts away from the Zuma era of despondency. It is basically about stopping the loot and reinstating some of the basic functions of public institutions. It is a matter of freeing the institutions from capture and allowing them to breathe a little. This does not require innovation in terms of design and so on. All it requires is that the leader stops interfering in the institutions and allows them to perform their basic functions. For this purpose, Ramaphosa is a sure winner. If it was not for the fact that he is a hands-on person, Ramaphosa could merely fold his arms and allow for the natural return of institutions to normality. He might have to do some tinkering with governance. Yet, even that is not necessary for him to help the ANC win the 2019 elections.

Let us consider, in this regard, what it took for the elite police unit, the Hawks, to galvanise themselves into action in pursuing their investigations into the Vrede dairy farm scandal involving the

Gupta family.[64] Once it was clear that the tide had turned against Zuma, and barely two months after Ramaphosa was elected president of ANC, the Hawks began arresting people implicated in the Vrede scheme. By the time Ramaphosa was inaugurated as president on 15 February, the Hawks had already announced concrete steps relating to the prosecution of these accused. Looking at the nature and depth of the alleged crimes involved, it is clear that the investigations must have been under way at least for some time before Ramaphosa was elected ANC president. This shows that the Hawks were already sitting on sufficient evidence to charge the culprits months before they actually did so. When the Hawks scaled up their investigations, they were merely toeing the line laid down by the new leadership of the ANC.

Should Ramaphosa take credit for the Hawks' investigations into the Vrede farm scandal? Why not? If the police and the prosecution authority suddenly realise that to keep in favour with Ramaphosa and protect their jobs they have to arrest the bad guys, so be it. The nation will at least gain from this calculation by public servants. Thus, in general terms, given the positive public mood that Ramaphosa has brought to the country, all he has to do is simply take a position on any issue that communicates the message that he is not Zuma. The rest will automatically follow. Public servants might even start showing up at their jobs with greater inspiration

---

64   "Explosive indictment in Vrede dairy farm case implicates Zwane, Magashule", *City Press*, 15 February 2018. Available at: https://city-press.news24.com/News/explosive-indictment-in-vrede-dairy-farm-case-implicates-zwane-magashule-20180215 (accessed 15 February 2018).

to carry out their daily duties, now that they sense they are part of the"new dawn".

But even where conditions are favourable to politicians, as seems to be the case with Ramaphosa, own goals can be scored and this can upset the game plan altogether. The worst thing Ramaphosa could do under the favourable circumstances in which he finds himself is to get involved in unnecessary confrontations before the 2019 elections. There is no need for risky experimentations before a full political mandate can be conferred on him in 2019. From his inauguration in February 2018 until elections are held in 2019, Ramaphosa has to demonstrate the art of waiting.

In my view, therefore, it was quite unnecessary of Ramaphosa's government to hike VAT as a way of restoring South Africa to a sound fiscal trajectory. This is a battle he could have deferred to a much later time, after the elections. After all, this policy may not have any significant impact by the time elections are held, save for asset managers, who have already started reaping the rewards of a positive economic outlook since the VAT announcement was made in the 2018 budget. When it comes to addressing the crisis of confidence in the economy, the VAT hike was a milestone that would bear immediate results. But for ordinary people who live in the real world, as opposed to the world of economic gimmicks, it is highly unlikely that the VAT increase will positively improve their economic standing by the time the elections are held in 2019.

This step, moreover, brings Ramaphosa into an unnecessary confrontation with the trade unions and the opposition parties, including the DA. Why should Ramaphosa incur liability from a policy whose success will not help him and his party in the forthcoming elections? Well, perhaps this is about principles.

Ramaphosa may want to demonstrate that he is taking a principled and non-populist position regarding the economy. Are we seeing here an unbridled sense of self-confidence by Ramaphosa or does he genuinely believe he has to carry this out? There is a thin line between bravery and stupidity. As mentioned earlier, the alliance partners COSATU and the SACP took exception to the VAT hike, indicating their misgivings about how Ramaphosa is burdening the broader society with the fiscal problem created by the ANC government under Zuma. Former COSATU general secretary Zwelinzima Vavi was quite scathing in depicting Ramaphosa's leadership as shielding the private sector at the expense of workers. In expressing the sense that Ramaphosa is protecting big business, Vavi said, "They have no worries whatsoever; they [now] know more than before that their mines, monopoly industries, the oceans and even the land will remain firmly in their hands."[65] This was the first indictment of Ramaphosa's policies since he became president. Vavi's view resuscitates the perception that Ramaphosa will always do what he can to protect big business. There is no doubt that Ramaphosa will have to deal with this perception throughout his presidency. But there was no reason for him to ignite this battle prematurely.

A further indication that the VAT hike was a blunder was shown in the manner in which the DA responded. It is important to note that the DA's position regarding tax increases is always the standard liberal line that there should be a reduction of corporate tax

---

65   J. Evans, "Vavi warns workers to avoid 'butcher of the working class' after budget", *Mail & Guardian*, 24 February 2018. Available at: https://mg.co.za/article/2018-02-25-vavi-warns-workers-to-avoid-butcher-of-the-working-class-after-budget (accessed 24 February 2018).

to ensure that companies thrive and employ more people.[66] As other observers have also noted, I don't buy the idea that if you put more money in the pockets of rich people, somehow it will emerge in the pockets of the poor. I don't believe in magic. The DA's logic concludes that, instead of punishing all South Africans for the ANC's sins, it is better to cut corporate tax. I don't understand this position either. It is the oddest political position, which shows how increasingly confused the party has become under the leadership of Mmusi Maimane. The only thing that made sense to me about the DA's response to the VAT proposal was that the party realised it could also extract a few drops of political juice by opposing this move. The DA initiated a petition to oppose the VAT increase on the basis that it is unduly punitive of the poor. A shrewd move.

It appears that as the political well that nourished the DA and other opposition parties under Zuma dried up when Ramaphosa was inaugurated, they saw the VAT increase as the first opportunity to remind South Africans that there is still room for the opposition parties under Ramaphosa. Once again, Ramaphosa did not have to provide this avenue for them before obtaining a more meaningful popular mandate in the 2019 elections. I am of the view that a VAT increase is such a severe measure that no one should attempt it without first gauging the strength of his or her mandate.

In general, doing too much too hastily will spell trouble for Ramaphosa, whose power base within the ANC is shakier than

---

66 "Fault line between DA and EFF: To hike corporate tax or not #Budget 2018", *702*, 22 February 2018. Available at: http://www.702.co.za/articles/293064/ fault-line-between-da-and-eff-to-hike-corporate-tax-or-not-budget2018 (accessed 24 February 2018).

we are willing to admit. As far as the 2019 elections are concerned, Ramaphosa stands a good chance of delivering victory for the ANC, unless he severely botches it. If we look at how his presidency is intensely lobbied by and largely crafted through corporate interest – he is regarded as the most economically sound man since the end of apartheid – it is of concern when he takes political risks that show he is comfortable in erring on the side of corporate interests, while displaying ambivalence and expressing caution about pro-gressive social policies.

For Ramaphosa to retain favour within the progressive civil society and social movements in the country, he has to become something of a Robin Hood: that is, willing to take from the rich and give to the poor. While the broader society seems to love him unconditionally, Ramaphosa should note that he cannot be seen to be forgiving in his attitude towards corporate South Africa. If, moreover, his policies can unite such diverse parties as the DA, the EFF and COSATU, then the president needs to reconsider who his core constituents are. Leaders should avoid offending the poor, for instance, by forcing them to bear the cost of economic adventures carried out by the business elites and their political counterparts. Overall, instead of staging unnecessary battles like VAT, Rama-phosa should rather find comfort in the fact that he handled Zuma's exit well. All he really has to do now is to wait out the transition period without making crucial mistakes and gear himself up for the elections.

The manner in which Ramaphosa was portrayed throughout his campaign to lead the ANC was such that he is a dead-certain winner in the 2019 elections. He is a man of integrity, and he presents the ANC with an opportunity to redeem itself from the corrupt Zuma years. For some, he is deserving and wise enough to become president without having to bother with elections. This is how I believe South Africans feel about Ramaphosa's inauguration as interim president following Zuma's departure. But the fact is that Ramaphosa's mandate has not been tested with the general public. He did not take the ANC to the elections and win just yet; he became president through an internal party succession manoeuvre, which largely excluded participation of the broader nation.

After his victory at Nasrec, Ramaphosa could either have waited out the interim period before carrying the party to victory in 2019 or opt for the Zimbabwean route and go straight to the Union Buildings. To my surprise, he went the Zimbabwean route. The Zimbabwean route involves a change of national leadership by way of an internal party shuffle, notably without having to go to elections. When Robert Mugabe's fellow party members used the military to overturn his government and force him out in November 2017, the old man realised the military had no willingness to complete the coup d'état against him. They needed his resignation so that they could dispense with the risk of elections. During that time, Mugabe held the military brass to ransom because he knew they required his signature to form a new government without having to refresh the government's mandate through elections.[67]

What makes the Zimbabwean transition interesting is that a similar manoeuvre was undertaken in South Africa, minus the involvement of the military, of course. Both ZANU-PF and the ANC

---

67 "Zimbabwe declares Mugabe's birthday a holiday", *News24*, 27 November 2017. Available at: https://www.news24.com/Africa/Zimbabwe/zimbabwe-declares-mugabes-birthday-a-holiday-20171127 (accessed 28 November 2017).

managed to contain an internal party falling-out within the party, and imposed a leader upon the nation without proper consultation with the general public. Even more disturbingly similar about the two cases is that both nations were so disgruntled with the ousted leaders that they were prepared to accept any kind of change of government, even if that was not ideal in terms of democratic principles.

Zuma was also placed under siege by the ANC leadership then stewarded by Ramaphosa. During the time when negotiations for Zuma's exit were under way, it became clear that the ANC wanted to ensure that the transition was managed internally within the party. Above all, the party wanted to avoid a parliamentary process such as a no-confidence motion that could see Zuma being voted out. This would strengthen the call for early elections, which would be risky for the ANC. Had a motion of no confidence in Zuma been passed in Parliament, the opposition parties would have approached the courts to make a case for the need to refresh the ANC's political mandate and hold early elections. A debilitated ANC then just escaping Zuma's hold would not have done well in elections so soon.

The irony in all this was Zuma's response to calls for him to resign. Zuma insisted that the "people still love him"[68] and said that he did not understand why he should resign. Given the fact

---

68   M. Malefane and N. Goba, "'People still want me as president': Zuma", *Sowetan Live*, 8 February 2018. Available at: https://www.sowetanlive.co.za/news/south-africa/2018-02-06-people-still-want-me-as-president-zuma/ (accessed 10 February 2018).

that the ANC performed poorly in the 2016 local government elections, Zuma's claim was debatable. In the 2016 local government elections, the ANC lost control of the key metro municipalities of Tshwane, Johannesburg and Nelson Mandela Bay. Zuma did not come out of these elections with a strong mandate. Therefore, he was either dishonest or delusional in his claim that the people loved him; but he was correct in terms of the principle that leaders should test their mandate with the people through elections.

Indeed, there should have been elections before Ramaphosa assumed his duties as the president of the country. Of course, our Constitution allows that Parliament can elect an interim president if the situation so dictates. There is nothing illegal about what happened. However, this approach has problematic political implications and it might also be used to raise concerns about the basis for Ramaphosa's sweeping policy changes. He could be seen as implementing a mandate he has not yet properly obtained. For the most part, however, except for the EFF's boycott of Ramaphosa's nomination in Parliament,[69] most South Africans are just happy to no longer have an embarrassing president like Zuma.

Going straight to the Union Buildings before the elections, and undertaking sweeping policy positions such as the VAT increase, would under normal circumstances work against Ramaphosa as he takes his party to the 2019 elections. But these things do not matter

---

69 "EFF says will boycott election of new president Thursday", *Moneyweb*, 15 February 2018. Available at: https://www.moneyweb.co.za/news-fast-news/eff-says-will-boycott-election-of-new-president-thursday/ (accessed 15 February 2018).

because they are about the substance of policy, and Ramaphosa's performance has been predominantly judged from the point of view of the country's crisis of confidence.

About ten days after his presidential inauguration, polls were already indicating that Ramaphosa could secure a 70% victory for the ANC in 2019. That's a good start, but a lot can still happen between now and then.

The biggest challenge Ramaphosa in fact faces is not from the opposition parties, but from opposition within his own party, the ANC. This requires that Ramaphosa's efforts to gear up for the elections are always at par with his efforts to stabilise the ANC and build a reliable power base to ensure he can make decisions without wider resistance from his fellow comrades. That balance could have been achieved by spending more time stabilising the party and nursing the wounds inflicted at the bruising elective conference, instead of going straight to the Union Buildings as president of the country.

It would have been better perhaps for Ramaphosa to remain a powerful deputy president who still called the shots. In that way, Ramaphosa could have avoided taking direct responsibility for some of the problems inherited from Zuma that may still unfold up to the time of the 2019 elections. Investigations into state capture will require that the president takes responsibility for some of the revelations that will most likely emerge. By assuming the office of the president, Ramaphosa has inadvertently acquired the role of having to protect some of his fellow "top six" ANC leaders who may have to respond to allegations of actively participating in the process of state capture. Already, fingers have been pointed at Jessie Duarte[70] and Ace Magashule in this regard.[71]

By not allowing for a cooling-off period before stepping into the Union Buildings, Ramaphosa has exposed himself to the standard criticism within the ANC: namely using state institutions to fight political battles within the party. It is well known that Ramaphosa's campaign to lead the ANC stood for almost everything that Magashule and Duarte did not. Consequently, if state institutions such as the police and prosecution services do their jobs and pursue those figures, Ramaphosa will be accused of resorting to the presidency to get this done. Had he avoided the temptation of becoming president, Ramaphosa would have been able to distance himself from the charge that he was using state institutions to evict Magashule and Duarte from the ANC. This could trigger a serious backlash within the ANC, which might expose Ramaphosa's vulnerability within the party and damage the public belief that he can steer the ANC in the right direction. As I indicated, the ultimate goal for Ramaphosa should be to avoid any unnecessary backlash before the elections, both within and outside the party.

The decision to become the president of the country before the 2019 elections also brought Ramaphosa into an uncomfortable proximity to David Mabuza, his deputy president. Not only is

70   M. Magome, "Duarte 'didn't get son-in-law a job'", *Independent Online*, 17 February 2016. Available at: https://www.iol.co.za/business-report/economy/duarte-didnt-get-son-in-law-a-job-1985618 (accessed 19 December 2017).

71   A. Umraw, "A round-up of Ace Magashule's son's Gupta connections", *Huffington Post*, 23 January 2018. Available at: http://www.huffingtonpost.co.za/2018/01/23/a-round-up-of-ace-magashules-sons-gupta-connections_a_23340902/ (accessed 25 January 2018).

Mabuza an election liability for the ANC, but his presence next to Ramaphosa raises questions about the meaning of anti-corruption within the ANC and whether Ramaphosa has any real power within the party. Opposition parties will have a field day with Mabuza as deputy president. Of great concern to me is that this problem could have been avoided – unless Ramaphosa has a plan to rehabilitate Mabuza's image in time before the 2019 elections.

Had he patiently waited his turn, Ramaphosa would have cruised to the 2019 elections and then easily attained the necessary majority to implement his agenda. Perhaps the thinking behind his acceptance of the presidency immediately after the party's Nasrec conference might have had to do with his belief that some progress could be achieved before the elections. This could conceivably place the ANC on a recovery route. Let me emphasise again that in my view this is an unnecessary adventure that seems to attract more risks than returns for Ramaphosa.

If, as the result of Ramaphosa's doing, the ANC attains a very strong majority in 2019 (over 60%), there is nothing to prevent some within the party from plotting against him. A strong majority could lead some in the party to believe that they don't really need him to hold on to power. A strong majority, moreover, will be of little use to Ramaphosa and his agenda. An ANC that has a strong majority is dangerous not only for Ramaphosa, but also for the country, as the party would not feel an obligation to bargain and compromise on some of its policies. What Ramaphosa needs in order to keep the ANC in check is a weaker majority, which will also allow him to innovate as a way of increasing the party's electoral hold. South Africa's politics require a reinstatement of the spirit of bargaining when it comes to policies. A strong majority for the ANC, on the other hand, will not create the space for this approach.

The 2019 elections are not only about the national picture; they are also about the power play at provincial level. As much as the ANC's reputation at national level is on the mend following Ramaphosa's inauguration, the provinces have their own dynamics which need to be looked at individually. Power is national, but it is also local and regional first. Gauteng, the Western Cape and Eastern Cape are some of the provinces where the ANC is experiencing completely different electoral dynamics from what is seen at national level. Then again, the first two contain some of the larger metropolitan municipalities, where the political dynamism is demonstrably higher than what is found in other parts of the country.

If there are lessons to be learned from the 2016 local government elections, it is that political shifts in the country are most likely to begin in the metropolitan areas before the domino effect is felt at provincial and ultimately at national government level. This was indicated when the ANC failed to secure an outright majority in the metropolitan municipalities of Tshwane, Johannesburg and Nelson Mandela Bay.[72] All the metropolitan municipalities lost by the ANC in 2016 constitute an important barometer when it comes to gauging how much support the ANC might be able to retain in those provinces in which these municipalities are found.

If the ANC could lose Tshwane and Johannesburg together, then

---

72   T. Khaas, "ANC's big loss", *City Press*, 23 August 2016. Available at: https:// city-press.news24.com/Voices/ancs-big-loss-20160819 (accessed 23 August 2016).

the party is facing a serious risk of losing Gauteng province some-time in the near future. The same goes for Nelson Mandela Bay and the Eastern Cape. The same sequence of events defines what took place in the Western Cape, where the ANC's losing streak began with the loss of the City of Cape Town in 2006. The province was subsequently surrendered by the ANC to the DA in 2009. It will take a great deal of work for the ANC to win back the Western Cape, despite the internal leadership battles that are consuming the DA in that province.[73] For now, the prospect of recovery for the ANC is not on the horizon in the Western Cape.

Gauteng will be interesting to watch. There is a real chance that the ANC may not be easily forgiven for some of its failures in the province. The tragedy of Life Esidimeni, which resulted in the death of 144 psychiatric patients in institutions in Gauteng,[74] will have left a bitter taste in the mouths of residents. It will take a great deal of work for Ramaphosa to put the ANC on a recovery journey here towards the 2019 elections. The work is doable, but Gauteng remains one of the provinces where opposition parties invest great efforts in poking holes in the "good" story that the ANC keeps on reciting.

Gauteng also is home to the urban radicalism of the black mid-

73   R. Davis, "Tensions revealed in DA Western Cape as leadership battle looms", *Daily Maverick*, 4 October 2017. Available at: https://www.dailymaverick.co.za/article/2017-10-04-tensions-revealed-in-da-western-cape-as-leadership-battle-looms/#.WpU9AuhuY2w (accessed 6 November 2017).

74   "Four patients located out of 59 missing Life Esidimeni patients", *The Citizen*, 31 January 2018. Available at: https://citizen.co.za/news/south-africa/1801801/four-patients-located-out-of-59-missing-life-esidimeni-patients/ (accessed 31 January 2018).

dle class, to whom and on whose behalf no political party speaks directly. For example, the EFF's radical economic transformation policy does not deal with the problem of the increasing tax burden that the middle class is confronted with. As for the DA, the party's anti-corruption crusade is not a basis for the identity politics that the black middle class still yearns for. Judging by the way they often respond to incidents of racism, members of the black middle class still consider themselves disadvantaged due to their race.

The ANC has had big differences with the middle class in recent years, often casting this group as an ungrateful beneficiary of the party's progressive agenda.[75] For its part, the black middle class has been more embarrassed by some of the offences committed by the ANC government under Zuma than, say, the poor, who still see the ANC as the only party with a commitment to dispensing social welfare in the country.[76] Unlike the poor, who are still concerned mostly with bargaining for basic services from the ANC, the middle class is still caught up in identity politics. Therefore, when the ANC gets caught in maladministration and corruption, the black middle class is more offended, particularly when these issues are used by whites to reflect on the broader question of black leadership. Political misdemeanours by the opposition parties do not hurt

---

75   C. du Plessis, "ANC woos black middle class", *Mail & Guardian*, 1 April 2016. Available at: https://mg.co.za/article/2016-03-31-anc-woos-black-middle-class (accessed 19 June 2017).

76   M. wa Azania, "Why the poor vote for the ANC and will do so for a long time", *Mail & Guardian (Thought Leader)*, 9 September 2013. Available at: http://thoughtleader.co.za/malaikawaazania/2013/09/09/why-the-poor-vote-for-the-anc-and-will-do-so-for-a-long-time/ (accessed 12 November 2017).

the middle class as much as when those mistakes emanate from the ANC. This is because the ANC has a historical obligation to protect the idea of black excellence against any racist onslaught. When the actions of the ANC dent the idea that black people can lead and run things properly, the ANC severely offends the black middle class.[77] Can Ramaphosa rekindle this relationship?

It will take more than eloquence for the black middle class to believe in the ANC's "good story to tell". Despite his contentious relationship with the private sector, Ramaphosa will most likely avoid actively offending the black middle class. The challenge also lies in how the ANC responds internally to his leadership. If ANC leaders openly defy Ramaphosa and question his authority, the middle class will not believe that the ANC is on the mend. All the same, Ramaphosa is the closest members of the black middle class will ever get to someone who at times speaks like them.

The 2019 elections will also be a battle for the attention of the poor. It emerged in the 2016 local government elections that the majority of poor people were losing interest in voting.[78] The opposite experience was seen in relation to the middle class and the rich: they showed up in greater numbers during the 2016 local government elections, mostly to vote for the DA. The 2016 elections could have signalled that the opposition parties, particularly

---

77 R. Southall, *The New Black Middle Class in South Africa*. Johannesburg: Jacana Media, 2016.

78 P. Herman, "ANC's 'lost 3 million voters' will decide 2019 elections: Tony Leon", *News24*, 24 August 2016. Available at: https://www.news24.com/SouthAfrica/News/ancs-lost-3-million-voters-will-decide-2019-elections-tony-leon-20160824 (accessed 12 November 2017).

the DA, have exhausted their electoral support base. If the opposition parties failed then to bridge the ANC's electoral base in the middle of Zuma's disastrous administration, it is difficult to imagine that they will achieve this when Ramaphosa heads the ANC.

The task that the ANC is faced with in the run-up towards the 2019 elections is not to regain voters who have left the party for the opposition, but simply to activate disgruntled voters who left the party to sit in the "transit lounge". This is where most of the ANC voters – the poor and some quarters of the black middle class – have gathered to seek shelter from Zuma's hail of corruption. These are the voters that Ramaphosa himself can reactivate with minimal effort by simply not being Zuma.

Even if the road to the 2019 elections seems to be wide open for Ramaphosa, there is always the chance that things will go awry. For example, it is necessary that the ANC consolidates provincial leadership before going into the elections, to ensure that the party's election machinery is fully functional. I am one of those who believe that political power in South Africa is dispersing from the national level and becoming concentrated at regional and local level. The ANC went into its elective conference at Nasrec against the backdrop of an intense provincial consolidation of power that influenced the outcome of the national leadership battle. The rise of the "Premier League" as a power base[79] is a stark indication of the importance of regional and provincial spaces as a means to access power

---

79   R. Munusamy, "ANC's leadership race: The rise of the 'premier league'", *Daily Maverick*, 7 September 2015. Available at: https://www.dailymaverick.co.za/article/2015-09-07-ancs-leadership-race-the-rise-of-the-premier-league/#.WpVB3ehuY2w (accessed 2 November 2017).

in the ANC. Consequently there may be a more intense power battle in provincial and regional structures of the party as we get closer to the 2019 elections. If not properly managed, those power struggles may undermine the provinces' abilities to campaign. If a sizeable part of the ANC in Kwazulu-Natal, for example, decides not to campaign alongside Ramaphosa, this would bear negative consequences on the party's performance. It is important that provinces such as KZN are brought in line by ensuring leadership coherence.

If the ANC succeeds in activating its disgruntled voters who were lost during the 2016 local government elections, the voter turnout in 2019 will most likely be higher than was seen in the 2014 general elections.[80] Ramaphosa may find it easy to strike up a conversation with some of the black middle class, the working class and the corporate sector. But this does not guarantee that his message will be heard by rural voters. As the ANC has been losing its legitimacy among urban voters, the party will be looking to obtain a bigger number of rural votes so as to return to power in government.

---

80   IEC, "2014 national and provincial elections: National results". Available at: http://www.elections.org.za/content/Elections/Results/2014-National-and-Provincial-Elections--National-results/ (accessed 12 November 2017).

8.

Playing the Rural Voter Game

～～

If the ANC will be in power until Jesus comes, as Jacob Zuma once claimed, then Jesus will probably arrive earlier in the urban areas than in the rural areas of South Africa. For while the ANC is still holding up in the rural areas, the party is experiencing rapid voter loss in urban centres. Within the top leadership of the ANC, the fear is that the party could become a "rural party". Responding to the party's poor performance in key urban centres during the 2016 local government elections, the ANC's national chairperson stated, "We're working to regain lost ground, we don't want to be relegated to a rural party. We want to regain the metros."[81] This

---

81 G. Davis,"Mantashe: ANC can't afford to become a rural party", *Eyewitness News*, 18 December 2017. Available at: http://ewn.co.za/2017/12/18/ mantashe-anc-can-t-afford-to-become-a-rural-party (accessed 9 January 2018).

tendency to face a path of decline is common to many liberation political parties: they gradually become rural parties, as we have seen in Zimbabwe, where ZANU-PF remains quite strong in the rural areas after losing ground in urban centres. This is the reason why the best thing the ANC can do to minimise the impact of urban voter losses on the party's national electoral share is to focus efforts on maintaining rural support. This is not an easy task because of the complexity of rural voters in South Africa, as I will show in this chapter. A rural vote is not a given for the ANC, and the party will need to understand that it takes effort to win the hearts of rural voters, who are becoming more and more informed and increasingly thinking twice before casting their votes.

With the 2019 elections looming in South Africa, there is a compelling case for the ANC to start to reach out to rural voters in a focused way. I do not think the ANC has previously concerned itself with the specifics of the rural vote. Until the 2016 local government elections heralded the urban revolt against the ANC, the party did not really focus on specific issues relating to rural voters as a distinct voting bloc. The ANC then still enjoyed wide political support across the country, in a way that did not show up the rural-urban divide. The picture will most likely change in the 2019 elections, when the party's chances of retaining support nationally may just depend on the rural vote, particularly in the rural-based provinces such as Limpopo, North West and Mpumalanga as well as the rural parts of KwaZulu-Natal and the Eastern Cape. The rural vote may very well determine the fate of those elections. How will the ANC craft its message to attract the rural vote in 2019?

In the village where I grew up in Limpopo, Bochum, it was

completely unthinkable for anyone to identify with the DA a decade ago. Most people in the rural areas could only wear ANC T-shirts in public. I do not recall seeing anyone wearing a DA shirt. Today, not only do people openly wear the blue DA shirts, but a person might wear an ANC shirt on the weekend, an EFF shirt during the week, and the DA shirt whenever the ANC and EFF shirts are in the laundry. On any given day, one can see different shirts on display, showing the influence of different political parties. The reality, however, is that the majority of the people in the villages still vote for the ANC. Still, there is nothing that stops them from bargaining for maximum returns from the ANC by threatening to vote for other political parties such as the EFF and the DA.

This is not often acknowledged in the public discourse in South Africa because of the dominant view that rural voters are only concerned with parochial politics. This is not true, for various reasons. Rural voters also engage in a cost-benefit analysis when voting, although they are confronted with circumstances different from those of their urban counterparts. Secondly, there aren't many differences between the majority of urban voters and their rural counterparts when it comes to how they relate to the ANC.[82] The distinction between rural and urban voters in South Africa is at best superficial. It is dominated by the view that in a modern democratic dispensation everyone is destined to live in the urban areas.

---

82   S. Friedman,"South Africans in rural areas are saying 'no more': Why it matters", *The Conversation*, 8 November 2017. Available at: https://theconversation.com/ south-africans-in-rural-areas-are-saying-no-more-why-it-matters-87028 (accessed 9 January 2018).

Therefore, rural voters are seen as occupying the last remaining outposts of a disappearing way of life that will inevitably succumb to the urban way of living. This view holds that in the rural areas we find primitive communities whose value system – and presumably their political identities and preferences – are entirely shaped by a pre-modern way of life. Rural communities, in this view, are understood as inherently isolated, lacking meaningful contact with the dynamic economic and social world experienced in urban centres. The rural dweller is often lampooned as backward, unintelligent when it comes to voting,[83] conservative on social issues, superstitious and opposed to rational mentalities,[84] culturally averse to modernity, and tied to the traditional leadership of the chiefs – thus revealing their unfamiliarity with democracy.[85]

The belief that rural communities are totally cut off from urban centres is no longer true. Increasingly across many societies, rural communities can no longer be said to be significantly isolated from the cities and towns. In South Africa, for example, rural communities have long been in touch with their urban counterparts through the migrant labour system. Under the apartheid system, blacks were relegated to homelands and thus were not allowed to maintain

---

83   J.G. Gamble, "The rural side of the rural-urban gap", *Journal of Political Science and Politics*, 39, 3, 2006.

84   J.C. Pratt, *The Rationality of Rural Life*. Amsterdam: Harwood Academic Publishers, 1994.

85   L. Ntsebeza, "Rural governance and citizenship in post-1994 South Africa: Democracy compromised?", in J. Danielsand R. Southall (eds), *State of the Nation: South Africa 2004–2005*. Cape Town: HSRC Press, 2005.

permanent residency in urban centres,[86] despite often being fully employed there. While blacks are now allowed to reside permanently wherever they wish as citizens in a democratic society, the practice of maintaining a permanent home in the rural areas and a semi-permanent home in the urban areas continues. This dual presence makes it difficult to imagine rural sites that are totally isolated from the urban areas. There is a constant interaction and exchange between rural and urban communities. In a sense, there is a significant part of the population in South Africa that exists both as rural dwellers and as urban dwellers simultaneously.

In addition, the increase in mass media, particularly the access to mobile phones and other mass media devices and outlets, means that people in rural areas are able to consume near-similar information to urban communities, although on a lesser scale because of the high costs of data.[87] At present, all African countries are experiencing a rapid growth in cellphone ownership.[88] There is now greater access to smartphones with the capability to connect to mass media platforms such as Facebook, for example. Even if rural communities may show a lag when it comes to the dynamism and cultural shifts that characterise their urban counterparts, they

---

86   The Group Areas Act of 1950.

87   T. Mohapi, "Why do South Africans pay such high costs for mobile data?", *Mail & Guardian*, 31 March 2017. Available at: https://mg.co.za/article/2017-03-31-00-why-do-south-africans-pay-such-high-costs-for-mobile-data (accessed 27 November 2017).

88   "Mobile phones are transforming Africa", *The Economist*, 10 December 2016. Available at: https://www.economist.com/news/middle-east-and-africa/21711511-mobile-phones-are-transforming-africa-where-they-can-get-signal-mobile-phones (accessed 4 October 2017).

almost always have a sense of the pulse of urban life and politics, which they tend to emulate as they engage in their local struggles in the peripheries. An example of this is the growing trend of service delivery protests in rural communities, mirroring what has taken place in urban areas. The decision by the ANC government under Zuma to ban the broadcast of service delivery protests through the state-owned South African Broadcasting Corporation (SABC) was a stark admission by the ruling party that trends in urban areas do affect attitudes in rural areas.[89]

Unlike older, pre-modern societies, modern communities are more plugged in and in constant interaction with each other's experiences. In this way, rural areas in South Africa are not entirely quarantined from the trends experienced in urban centres. The idea of a rural vote is therefore more complex than is usually admitted in public discussions. People in urban areas tend to believe that they understand the dynamics of what they consider rural politics. In their view, rural voters are ignorant and vote for the ANC mostly because the party offers social grants. According to this view, they therefore vote on the basis of a single issue[90] and are not seen as maximisers of returns in their voting habits.

There is no proof one can offer, however, that urban voters have more complex demands than rural voters, except to point to the

---

89   J. de Villiers, "Icasa nullifies SABC's editorial policy", *News24*, 9 March 2017. Available at: https://www.news24.com/SouthAfrica/News/icasa-nullifies-sabcs-editorial-policy-20170309 (accessed 7 October 2017).

90   "Grants helped keep ANC in power: Analyst", *News24*, 9 May 2017. Available at: https://www.news24.com/elections/news/grants-helped-keep-anc-in-power-analyst-20140509 (accessed 3 May 2017).

social and economic conditions that urban voters experience. While urban voters may see corruption as a major issue in their lives, rural voters may choose not to rank corruption higher than, say, social grants in deciding how to cast their vote. For them a rational choice would be to vote rather on the issue of social grants. We should be careful here about two distinct points. Firstly, a political system where politics are predominantly concentrated in urban areas will limit the choices and options for rural voters. Secondly, when confronted with a choice between two priorities that are presented as mutually exclusive, rural voters still make decisions which are rational for them based on their circumstances. Thirdly, we must remember that when it comes to voting as a way to secure a set of political goals, there is no perfect choice.[91]

Moreover, we need to take notice that voters who live in rural areas have begun to express their concerns about the priorities of political parties, specifically the ANC. Criticisms have been raised that urban voters receive much from the party while rural areas are neglected.[92] This implies that voters in rural areas have a sense of perspective when comparing the returns they get with what urban voters get. It is important also to note that rural voters want the same returns as urban voters. The difference between the two is that the political system presents urban voters with more political

---

91 A. Edlin, A. Gelman and N. Kaplan, "Voting as a rational choice: Why and how people vote to improve the well-being of others", *Rationality and Society*, 19, 3, 2017.

92 "The race: Rural voters question ANC's priorities – Research", *eNCA*, 19 October 2017. Available at: https://www.enca.com/south-africa/rural-voters-question-ancs-priorities-research (accessed 4 November 2017).

options than their rural counterparts. This is because the level of economic development in urban areas is such that political parties invest much of their resources and electoral efforts there compared to the rural areas. It is unfair, then, to look upon rural voters as a group of people who fail to exercise their choices properly. The choices that rural voters are confronted with flow from the very nature of neglect that rural areas have experienced historically in South Africa. The apartheid regime's policy of deliberately impoverishing the rural areas has become a structural problem such that rural communities remain trapped in poverty and are neglected even in a democratic system.

It would be unfair not to point out that rural voters are often presented with much more difficult choices than their urban counterparts. Whereas urban voters only have to choose between different political parties to decide how their interests can be maximised, rural voters also have to deal with the interests and demands of traditional authorities. Under the apartheid system, rural communities were placed under traditional authorities, which exerted political, social and economic control over them. The practical challenge in post-apartheid South Africa has been to reconcile traditional leadership with a democratic order based on the Constitution. The approach thus far has been to attempt to develop an "organic democracy" according to which "traditional leaders should be useful for as long as the extension of democratic local governance is not sufficient towards the rural areas".[93] Practically, this

---

93   P. Sithole and T. Mbele, "Fifteen year review on traditional leadership: A research paper", Pretoria: Human Sciences Research Council, 2008.

has meant that traditional authorities have competed for power and authority with local agencies of government, the latter being understood as part of the democratic institutional framework.

Because of the generally poor state of local government,[94] especially when it comes to the delivery of services, local government has encountered legitimacy problems, particularly in rural areas where the service delivery backlog is concentrated. Consequently, traditional authorities have regained their legitimacy as decision-making institutions and coordinators with local government when it comes to local development projects.[95] The failure of local government has also created an institutional vacuum, which traditional authorities have readily stepped in to fill. As a result of this resumption of legitimacy by traditional leaders, they have become important figures to be cultivated by the ANC, and have been given additional powers as a reward for their loyalty to the ANC-led government and their presumed ability to deliver their followers as voting fodder for the ruling party.

The political analyst Steven Friedman has written extensively[96] and critically about the manner in which the ANC government has used its authority to confer certain powers on traditional authori-

---

94   S. Koma, "The state of local government in South Africa: Issues, trends, and options", *Journal of Public Administration*, 45, 1, 2010.

95   G. Ashton, "Transforming the tragedies of local government failure in South Africa", South African Civil Society Information Service, 11 June 2013. Available at: http://sacsis.org.za/site/article/1689 (accessed 19 January 2017).

96   S. Friedman, "South Africans in rural areas are saying 'no more': Why it matters", *The Conversation*, 8 November 2017. Available at: https://theconversation.com/south-africans-in-rural-areas-are-saying-no-more-why-it-matters-87028 (accessed 12 December 2017).

ties, in a way that disempowers communities. Friedman points, for instance, to the proposed Traditional Leadership and Governance Framework Bill, "which essentially aims to give traditional leaders the power to strike mineral deals with private outside conglomerates to extract what is estimated to be R36 trillion ($2.5 trillion) of mineral reserves in rural areas".[97] According to Friedman, the bill will enrich traditional authorities at the expense of rural communities.

Within a properly functioning system of local government, traditional leaders are not essentially suspect. As I argued in my book *When Zuma Goes*,[98] there is nothing inherently wrong with traditional institutions. Indeed, there are opportunities for traditional leadership to evolve towards democratic practices. However, the quest for survival for both the ANC and traditional authorities comes at the expense of rural communities.

Having examined the nature of the rural voter, the question is: what might be President Cyril Ramaphosa's approach to rural communities? A simple answer is that he should try to avoid the example of former president Zuma. Zuma was the first president in democratic South Africa who deliberately sought to target rural communities as part of his political survival strategy. He patronised them and saw them as a way of neutralising his political opponents concentrated in the urban centres. Zuma spoke to rural communities in a way that sought to show how their issues were essentially in conflict with those prioritised by urban communities. When finding himself embattled in the rest of the country, Zuma responded

---

97   Ibid.

98   R. Mathekga, *When Zuma Goes*. Cape Town: Tafelberg, 2016.

by flaunting his ties with rural communities as a source of moral authority for his leadership. This does not necessarily mean that his political project of corruption was supported by rural voters. But he went after them all the same because of his belief that their perceived ignorance was a good basis for the political support he needed to stay in power. This is exactly what Ramaphosa's leadership ought to avoid: treating rural communities as readily accessible and cheap votes.

Ramaphosa has to speak to rural communities by recognising them as agents capable of full participation in the economy and society. Furthermore, Ramaphosa should avoid pitting rural communities against their urban counterparts. In substance, there is no meaningful difference between rural communities and urban communities as far as political goals are concerned. Both communities are interested in social and economic prosperity. The difference is that they engage in politics under different circumstances, and this also determines the choices presented to them.

Ramaphosa also needs to develop a clear idea of rural economic development. Perhaps he should take note of the talk in areas such as Gauteng about the "township economy", which has been championed by Gauteng premier David Makhura.[99] The Gauteng government's decision to adopt a township-focused economy as a policy intervention comes from the realisation that mainstream policies do not address the specific needs of the townships, which

---

99 "Gauteng leads the revitalization of township economies: Makhura", *The Citizen*, 28 February 2018. Available at: http://www.sabcnews.com/sabcnews/gauteng-leads-revitalisation-township-economies-makhura/ (accessed 28 February 2018).

are situated on the outskirts of the urban centres. The same approach needs to be adopted in relation to rural economies in South Africa. Ramaphosa needs to craft a policy that will deal with the specific challenges experienced in rural areas. Given the historical experience in which rural communities were deliberately impoverished under the apartheid system so they would remain labour reserves for the industrial urban centres, it should be obvious that without concerted targeted intervention, rural communities will always lag far behind the rest of the country when it comes to development.

The idea of a rural economy should not be reduced to small-scale farming or those undignified government-sponsored jobs such as the clearing of bushes alongside public roads. Although any employment is better than no employment, such jobs are unfulfilling. It is important for policy planners to be more imaginative when it comes to revitalising the rural economy. It is worrying, however, that despite the development gap experienced by rural areas, South Africa has yet to adopt a tax incentive system to encourage companies to invest in rural economies. China, for instance, has a focused tax system through which the country encourages enterprises to invest in agribusiness[100] in rural areas of the country.

The main difference between China and South Africa in terms of the pursuit of rural economic development is not only the fact

---

100   A. Ling and H. Zhou, "China continues rural support with agribusiness tax incentives", *China Business Review*, 16 October 2014. Available at: https://www.chinabusinessreview.com/china-continues-rural-support-with-agribusiness-tax-incentives/ (accessed 4 July 2017).

that the two countries are far apart when it comes to institutional capacity. China's policy makers also do not labour under the presumption that all rural dwellers are destined eventually to migrate to the urban centres. In China, rural communities are seen as self-sustainable economic sites. With a focused economic policy aimed at generating economic activities, those rural areas will eventually urbanise instead of uprooting and moving to the towns and cities. Their destiny is not in the current urban centres.

The same could be true for South Africa. Urbanisation in South Africa has tended to create social problems, consequently imposing a cost on the economy. South Africa's urban cities are home to a growing number of unemployable youths. Rapid urbanisation should therefore not be seen as a progressive channel towards human development for the majority of young people in the country. In his attempt to speak to rural communities, Ramaphosa needs to address the challenges of forced migration from rural to urban centres. But more than that, he needs to ensure that South Africa starts afresh and fully explores the opportunities to revitalise the rural economy in South Africa.

It is also important for urban communities in South Africa to learn to appreciate the struggles that rural communities are involved in. There is a growing level of insensitivity among urban South Africans towards the plight of rural people. The ability of urban communities to dominate narratives in society does not mean that they are more knowledgeable about the plight of the rural poor. Furthermore, rural communities do not require any form of political rescue by their urban counterparts.

Rural communities are also capable of defining their own struggles. They are equally capable of identifying the most optimal solution under circumstances where political interactions among parties fail to provide them with adequate or meaningful choices. Opposition political parties do not invest many resources in engaging rural communities, although they always bemoan the ANC's domination in those areas. This may have to do with the limited resources that opposition parties have at their disposal when it comes to campaigning. In cases where opposition parties are unable to maintain constant, direct interaction with rural communities, they can show their commitment to the plight of rural people by properly reflecting their concerns in Parliament and other national forums.

If the ANC is serious about radical economic transformation,[101] reaching out to rural communities to ensure their social and economic participation is the best way to go about it. Radical economic transformation should also entail a completely different way of thinking about the challenges that the country is experiencing. Reflecting on what should be done with the rural economy should be the first step. The rural economy is not about the Somali shopkeepers who operate convenience stores in the rural areas. There is also more to the rural economy than receiving social grants.

Rural communities have seen enough dancing and singing by politicians over the years, with Zuma topping the charts in this

---

101 T. Khubeka, "Mkhize calls for inclusion of rural community in SA economy", *Eye Witness News*, 17 November 2017. Available at: http://ewn.co.za/2017/11/17/ mkhize-calls-for-inclusion-of-rural-community-in-sa-economy (accessed 18 November 2017).

regard. Being the questionable singer and dancer that he is, Ramaphosa needs to focus on building a new relationship with the rural dwellers of South Africa. They may just ensure his survival and that of his party.

9.

The KwaZulu-Natal Headache

Cyril Ramaphosa's attempts to unite the ANC following a decade of bruising factional battles under former president Jacob Zuma are experiencing serious headwinds in KwaZulu-Natal. Shortly after the ANC's Nasrec elective conference, the ANC in KwaZulu-Natal started to intensify its resistance to any pressure to realign itself away from Zuma. For nearly ten years Zuma used his home province to bolster his power and retain control of the ANC amid general unhappiness about his leadership across the party and the country. Of all ANC formations that felt betrayed by the Nasrec results, the ANC in KwaZulu-Natal left the conference feeling the most aggrieved. The KwaZulu-Natal ANC has the greatest membership of all the provinces and has remained the most influential in swaying leadership contests within the party, notably securing Zuma's victory in both the 2007 and the 2012 elective conferences.

Throughout Zuma's tenure as president of the party, the ANC in KwaZulu-Natal remained a serious power-broker within the party. It was a great shock for many, therefore, when this province walked away from Nasrec with empty hands and not a single one of its candidates elected to the ANC's "top six".

Divisions within the ANC in KwaZulu-Natal weakened the province's influence on the national leadership in the period leading up to the Nasrec conference, with the emergence of an anti-Zuma faction in the province. Ramaphosa gained from these divisions by receiving support from the anti-Zuma group in the province. There were expectations that the Zuma-aligned faction in KwaZulu-Natal would consider realigning itself to Ramaphosa when Zuma's tenure as president ended. Logic dictated that since there would be no benefit in continuing with a faction whose raison d'être had been to defend the outgoing president, the ANC in KwaZulu-Natal would move on after Nasrec. It has now become clear that the results of the Nasrec conference, specifically the defeat of the Zuma faction, are considered only a temporary upset by that faction in the province. This group apparently plans to pursue a long-term strategy to reclaim their space within the party. For this faction, Ramaphosa is simply the first obstacle in their plan to return the ANC in KwaZulu-Natal to glory.

For Ramaphosa, the situation in KwaZulu-Natal is of great concern for at least two reasons. Firstly, the remnants of the Zuma faction in KwaZulu-Natal could cause him sleepless nights because they do have a realistic chance of challenging his power base sometime in the future and ultimately deposing him as the president of the ANC. This might seem unlikely, but it is not impossible, especially when taking into consideration the fact that the Premier League is disintegrating fast and cannot counter the advances of the KZN faction. Within the Premier League, it is only David Mabuza who seems to have a strong foothold after Zuma's exit as president. Mabuza has apparently chosen to align himself with Ramaphosa's faction, assuming the position of deputy president in the latter's cabinet. Mabuza has also publicly vowed to defend Ramaphosa's presidency, which he sees as a move towards unity in the ANC. While Mabuza is cosying up to Ramaphosa, both Ace Magashule and Supra Mahumapelo – the other members of the Premier League – are experiencing a serious backlash because of their relationship with the embattled Gupta family.

The state capture narrative has made Mahumapelo and Magashule very vulnerable, to the point where they have to use their political bases within the party to fight for political survival. As newly elected ANC secretary general, Ace Magashule is clearly out of his depth as he battles efforts by the Hawks to unearth corruption in the province he once led. While he was still the premier of the Free State, Magashule's office was raided by the Hawks as part of the investigations into the Vrede dairy farm project. Mahumapelo of the North West also had to play reluctant host to the Hawks, who raided his offices in March 2018 in connection with allegations of corruption in the supply of an IT system.[102] If there is any indication that the Hawks are beginning to smell the after-Zuma coffee, it is evident in the way they started pursuing Zu-

---

102   J. Chabalala, "Hawks raid Supra Mahumapelo's office", *Huffington Post*, 8 March 2018. Available at: https://www.huffingtonpost.co.za/2018/03/08/hawks-raid-supra-mahumapelos-office_a_23380197/ (accessed 15 April 2018).

ma's allies just as he was recalled as president. Mabuza seems to be the only former Zuma ally who is not having sleepless nights worrying about the Hawks knocking on his door. Despite widespread allegations that he is a thuggish politician, Mabuza has no specific case to answer in relation to corruption, at least at this point in time. As I write this, I am convinced that Mabuza has ditched the Premier League because of the credibility crisis with which its members are confronted as a result of their previous relationship with the Gupta family. The fragmentation of the Premier League could mean that the two embattled members of this group, Mahumapelo and Magashule, might have to go knocking on the door of the Zuma faction sometime soon in order to survive politically.

Since becoming the deputy president of the country, Mabuza has become isolated from the Premier League and there are no real benefits for him any longer in maintaining his relationship with the group. Mabuza no longer needs the league to ascend further in the ANC as he is already lined up for the highest position in the party. Ramaphosa's faction may have to reward him with this position for having assisted their candidate to win against Nkosazana Dlamini-Zuma at Nasrec. Mabuza has no reason to help the embattled Mahumapelo and Magashule in their fight to fend off corruption charges. Since he is convinced he will one day become the president of the ANC, he has to be seen to be distancing himself from those who are alleged to be involved in corruption. This means that Magashule and Mahumapelo have only one place to look for help in dealing with police investigations into their affairs with the Guptas. All this renders KwaZulu-Natal a strategic stage when it comes to fighting against the abuse of state resources, including law enforcement, to conduct political battles within the ANC. The script is ready, and it has been in rehearsal since Zuma took control of the ANC in 2007. The line goes like this: there are those who are trying to use state institutions to dislodge some of the ANC leaders who were elected to power at Nasrec. This is seen as an attempt at a final takeover of the ANC.

The fact that Zuma has to face corruption charges in KwaZulu-Natal makes things even more interesting. This adds fuel to the fire, by allowing Zuma to mobilise the larger part of the ANC in KwaZulu-Natal in defiance of the party's national leadership. Before Zuma's first court appearance on 6 April 2018, the ANC's national executive committee issued a statement urging members of the party not to wear ANC regalia when they went to court to support Zuma, and to support him in their individual capacity only. This statement was ill-advised in the sense that party leaders knew well that ANC members would not heed such a directive. When Zuma appeared in court, scores of ANC members proudly clad in party colours showed up. At this moment it was clear that Zuma still enjoyed great influence among certain sections of the ANC and that the national leadership of the ANC was not as powerful as it would like to be. The incident provided much-needed proof for Zuma supporters in KwaZulu-Natal that they still have a chance to regain control of their ANC, which has been "stolen" from them.

Clearly, the ANC in KwaZulu-Natal could become a strategic point for a palace revolution against Ramaphosa. The likes of Magashule and Mahumapelo will most likely regroup with the

KwaZulu-Natal Zuma enclave to fight for their own political survival and to stay out of jail. Reports have already surfaced indicating that the KwaZulu-Natal ANC is hatching a plan to get rid of Ramaphosa.[103] The provincial ANC is fully aware that Zuma desperately needs support in his fight against the corruption charges which have landed him in court. In return for supporting him, the ANC's provincial power barons hope that Zuma will, with the little power that he has left, help them secure their hold on patronage in the provincial government, including the big-budget metro of eThekwini (Durban). If Zuma's ally Sihle Zikalala loses the position of provincial chairperson, this would mean that the Zuma faction will have no chance of winning a national contest for the ANC leadership in the near future. Without its resource-rich patronage network in the provincial government, the Zuma faction in Kwa-Zulu-Natal will not be able to reclaim its influence on the composition of the ANC's national leadership.

There is a second reason why the turmoil in KwaZulu-Natal should be of great concern for Ramaphosa: its implications for the ANC's electoral fortunes in 2019. There are very few leaders who are able to survive after poor performances in elections. President Zuma is one of them, and this despite not only a poor electoral performance, but credibility crises due to revelations of corruption, and a poor record in government. More often than not, leaders tend to fall out with their political parties after they fare poorly in general

---

103 "KZN ANC slams reports over Zuma supporters 'secret talks'", *Independent Online*, 8 April 2018. Available at: https://www.iol.co.za/news/politics/kzn-anc-slams-reports-over-zuma-supporters-secret-talks-14316161 (accessed 15 April 2018).

elections. One of the things that Ramaphosa should be worried about is whether the KwaZulu-Natal ANC will be fully behind his campaign for 2019. There is the possibility that the ANC in Kwa-Zulu-Natal could split their vote in the 2019 elections: by voting for the ANC at provincial level, and for a different party at national level.[104] If this happens, it would mean that the ANC in KwaZulu-Natal in effect votes against Ramaphosa.

Because KwaZulu-Natal has the highest ANC membership of all the provinces, it controls a huge number of votes at national level. Thus, if the ANC in KwaZulu-Natal withholds its vote in significant numbers for the party at the national level, the result will be devastating for the ANC. If the ANC under Ramaphosa performs poorly at the national level owing to the outcome of the KwaZulu-Natal vote, this could provide the justification for the ANC in KwaZulu-Natal to demand Ramaphosa's recall.

The contest for the provincial leadership of the ANC in KwaZulu-Natal is intertwined with Zuma's plans to continue to use his power in the province to strong-arm the national leadership into helping quash the corruption charges against him and protect him in the course of the state capture inquiry. In this battle for support, Zuma fired the first salvo by embarrassing the leadership of the ANC when he successfully mobilised party members to turn out for his first court appearance. Whenever Zuma draws support from party members in his fight against corruption charges, Ramaphosa's efforts to usher in the "new dawn" in the ANC and in the country appear more and more futile. Ultimately, Zuma is making it very

---

104   Ibid.

difficult for Ramaphosa to unite the party.

The problem that Ramaphosa's leadership faces with the ANC in KwaZulu-Natal is not a unique situation. Many leaders face opposition from certain sections in their parties and, although it is challenging, it is something many leaders survive. Zuma survived throughout his presidency despite a hostile relationship with the ANC in Gauteng. Attempts to remove Zuma through the structures of the ANC were always repelled mainly through support from KwaZulu-Natal. It may never be the case that all ANC provinces will be in sync with the national leadership of the party. Even more interesting is that the national leadership of the ANC is no longer a monolith itself; it is more and more made up of individuals with conflicting interests. The problem with the ANC in KwaZulu-Natal is that the situation is multi-layered, with factional politics mixed up with ethnicity. Zuma has made no secret of his Zulu heritage and culture. He has enjoyed support from KwaZulu-Natal largely because of his ability to amplify his ethnic identity.

Having been credited for successfully mediating murderous political conflict in KwaZulu-Natal in the immediate post-apartheid years, Zuma knows at first hand the explosive power that is generated when political identities are mixed with ethnic identities in the specific setting of KwaZulu-Natal. He himself is willing to mobilise ethnic support for political purposes. The danger of this formula is that not only does it amount to a recipe for open violence and a return to the political bloodbath of the 1990s, but it also has the potential to unite various factions against Ramaphosa. The threat of uniting KwaZulu-Natal on the basis of ethnicity should therefore be of concern.

The decision by the ANC to expropriate land without compensation could also bear unintended consequences in KwaZulu-Natal. The impact of this decision on the Ingonyama Trust, through which King Goodwill Zwelithini holds vast tracts of land on behalf of the Zulu nation,[105] could provide another juncture for strengthening ethnic identity as a way of mobilising political activity in KwaZulu-Natal. If the ANC presses on with this policy, Ramaphosa will be confronted not only with the possibility of ANC factions coalescing against him in KwaZulu-Natal, but also with other parties in the province becoming involved in this delicate matter. This scenario has already become evident, as witness the actions of EFF members in KwaZulu-Natal in defying Julius Malema and insisting that he should apologise to the monarch after his statement that the Ingonyama Trust land should also be expropriated.[106] Such developments will make it difficult for Ramaphosa to pacify the ANC in KwaZulu-Natal.

The end of Zuma's legal woes – whichever way that end presents itself – will not mean that the Zuma faction in the province would submit to Ramaphosa's leadership. Zuma's predicament has only set in train a movement as in search of a new point of consolidation following his defeat at Nasrec. Piecemeal efforts to retrieve the situation, such as Ramaphosa's decision to include his former

105 B. Mthethwa, "Zulu monarch's warning to ANC over thorny land issue", *TimesLive*, 22 January 2018. Available at: https://www.timeslive.co.za/politics/2018-01-22-zulu-monarchs-warning-to-anc-over-thorny-land-issue/ (accessed 14 April 2018).

106 "EFF members chose Zulu king over Malema in KwaZulu-Natal", *The Citizen*, 14 April 2018. Available at: https://citizen.co.za/news/south-africa/1894521/4eff-members-choose-zulu-king-over-malema-in-KwaZulu-Natal/ (accessed 15 April 2018).

rival Nkosazana Dlamini-Zuma in his cabinet, have fallen short in appeasing the mutineers in KwaZulu-Natal. The inclusion of the KwaZulu-Natal heavyweight Zweli Mkhize in Ramaphosa's cabinet has also not earned him much goodwill in the province.

Had the ANC leadership under Ramaphosa achieved the impossible task of protecting Zuma from prosecution, the party might not be facing the same backlash in KwaZulu-Natal. Zuma understands the art of street politics, and his ability to mobilise support on the ground is unmatched in the ANC. The mere idea that the ANC in KwaZulu-Natal is considering using Zuma in campaigning for the 2019 elections appears to defy logic when one takes into account that the man is a suspect in a criminal case. When in trouble with the law, Zuma often turns out to be successful when it comes to mobilising support. This makes Ramaphosa's job in KwaZulu-Natal very complex and potentially dangerous. Whenever Zuma's allies have to face criminal charges arising from their dealings during his tenure, there will be a further consolidation of the anti-Ramaphosa group in KwaZulu-Natal. Ramaphosa finds himself between a rock and a hard place. In the improbable event that he considers protecting or even pardoning those implicated in corruption, his integrity ticket would be compromised and South Africans will lose trust in the idea of the "new dawn". If Ramaphosa looks away, as he should, when law enforcement goes after senior Zuma allies, he will still be accused of doing nothing to help his embattled comrades. It's a lose-lose situation for Ramaphosa.

No one anticipated the remnants of the Premier League – Mahumapelo and Magashule – rallying behind the KwaZulu-Natal pro-Zuma faction. This means that Ramaphosa can only rely on his own faction and on Mabuza to remain strong within the ANC. When Mabuza made an undertaking earlier in January 2018 – before Ramaphosa was inaugurated as president of the country – that he would support him, Mabuza already knew then that Ramaphosa would dearly need his support.

The best Ramaphosa can achieve in relation to the ANC in KwaZulu-Natal is to manage the crisis through a piecemeal approach. I do not think the ANC in KwaZulu-Natal will fully realign itself away from Zuma. Once Zuma's legal case is finalised, the former pro-Zuma group in KwaZulu-Natal will still push ahead to influence the outcome of the leadership contest for their own benefit at the party's next elective conference. The first major battle will be the contest for the provincial leadership. The provincial leadership is a means of accessing patronage in the province and a foundational stage in contesting the national leadership. The KwaZulu-Natal ANC's campaign is no doubt going to stretch into the next elective conference of the ANC, to be held in 2022. If poorly managed, it has the potential to paralyse the party for years to come.

10.

Ramaphosa and the State Capturers

———∿∿———

Cyril Ramaphosa's first "close shave" with state capture came when the controversial Gupta family's private jet was used to transport him on an official trip he undertook to Japan in August 2015 as deputy president of South Africa.[107] According to media reports, the jet had been procured by the Department of Defence, which is responsible for organising air transport for the president and the deputy president. Apparently, the Gupta family jet was leased through a private company that provided chartered aircraft when the Department of Defence sought an available plane. On hearing of its provenance, opposition parties, including the Democratic Alliance, began asking whether Ramaphosa was yet

---

107 Kobus Marais, "Why did Ramaphosa fly to Japan on Gupta jet?", *Politicsweb*, 26 August 2015. Available at: http://www.politicsweb.co.za/politics/why-did-ramaphosa-fly-to-japan-on-gupta-jet—kobus (accessed 21 November 2017).

another high-ranking politician in the country with links to the Gupta family.

Even before the GuptaLeaks of 2017 produced a flood of email evidence about the extent of the family's capture of the state, there had been mounting signs emerging in public over the years. Already in 2013 the media had carried reports of a private jet, carrying Indian guests to a Gupta family member's wedding in Sun City, that had been allowed to land at a military air force base outside Pretoria. We now know that the wedding was funded from money laundered through the Vrede dairy farm project in the Free State in which the Guptas had an interest; the scandal also implicated the Free State provincial government, led by its Zuma-aligned premier and the ANC's new secretary general, Ace Magashule.[108]

But 2015 seems to have been the year in which the Gupta family consolidated their influence on the direction, priorities and capacity of the state in South Africa. Their aim was to align the entire institutional framework of the state in the pursuit of the Guptas' interests. It was in 2015 that the family influence at the state-owned electricity-generating company Eskom intensified.[109] During that year, the Gupta family shook up the board of Eskom and installed their stooges. The consolidation of the Gupta interest also affected the state-owned entity the Passenger Rail Agency of South Africa

---

108 AmaBhungane and Scorpio, "#GuptaLeaks: How millions milked from FS government paid for Sun City wedding", *Eyewitness News*, 30 June 2017. Available at: http://ewn.co.za/2017/06/30/guptaleaks-how-millions-milked-from-free-state-govt-paid-for-sun-city-wedding (accessed 21 November 2017).
109 Linda Ensor, "Zola Tsotsi links Zuma to Eskom capture", *Business Day*, 22 November 2017.

(Prasa), one of the big spenders among state-owned corporations when it comes to purchasing hardware.[110] Through their influence on the board, the Gupta family ensured that Prasa would be run as a gravy express. As the examples of Eskom and Prasa show, state capture peaked in 2015. Thus, if the Guptas had been gradually acquiring a stake in South Africa Incorporated since Jacob Zuma assumed the role of chief executive in 2009, then 2015 marked the year in which the family staged a hostile takeover bid to acquire a controlling stake in the country. It was a big gamble by the family, and it became a do-or-die situation, an all-or-nothing scenario.

The significance of 2015 in relation to state capture is that the Guptas were becoming increasingly aware that Zuma was going to have to go at some point, either when his term of office as president came to an end or if the ANC decided to remove him before then. This meant that the Guptas had to seek out and promote a new chief executive to the head of their acquired empire, South Africa Incorporated. Even if Ramaphosa did not know that he was using a Gupta jet when he made his official trip to Japan in 2015, there is no doubt that the Gupta brothers were making their move to see if Ramaphosa, then a possible successor of Zuma, would join them in their corner.

After the story surfaced in the media that the Guptas provided the private jet for Ramaphosa's official trip, there were two choices left for him. Ramaphosa either had to pretend he was not aware of

---

110   Matthew le Cordeur, "Guptas deny trying to capture R51bn Prasa tender", *Fin24*, 19 January 2016. Available at: https://www.fin24.com/Economy/gup-tas-deny-trying-to-capture-r51bn-prasa-tender-20160619 (accessed 24 November 2017).

the attempt by the Guptas to secure him as a future ally in pursuing state capture, or he had to come out and totally reject the Guptas' approach. Because the Gupta email leaks had not yet surfaced in public, speculation about state capture still relied on bits and pieces of information reported episodically in the media. By that time, Ramaphosa was becoming an attractive focus of opposition to the Gupta project. Three months after the embarrassing flight to Japan, Ramaphosa deliberately chose to fly on a commercial plane when he made an official visit to the Iranian capital city, Tehran. In this way he acknowledged the problem of the Gupta family's undue influence in South Africa and at the same time publicly distanced himself from them.[111]

Though Ramaphosa's own private wealth certainly insulates him from the attractions of involvement in the Guptas' schemes, not all billionaires in South Africa have been able to avoid the Gupta net. Tokyo Sexwale, who with Cyril belongs to the same class of super-rich beneficiaries of black economic empowerment, was non-executive chairman of Trillian. This Gupta-linked company was implicated in rampant tender corruption at Eskom.[112] After news broke that Trillian was in fact used by the Guptas as a clearing house for money from Eskom, Sexwale instituted an inquiry into the matter. Sexwale has since taken a tough stance against state capture, and he has been able to rehabilitate his name.

---

111 T. Jika and P. Rampedi, "Cyril flies commercial after Gupta spat", *Sunday Times*, 1 November 2015.

112 A. Serrao, "NPA concludes Eskom payments to McKinsey and Trillian were criminal", *Fin24*, 17 January 2018. Available at: https://www.fin24.com/ Economy/npa-concludes-eskom-payments-to-mckinsey-and-trillian-were-criminal-20180117 (accessed 21 November 2017).

Sexwale's experience shows that state capture in South Africa was a war of all against all. One was either on the side that defended state capture for the reason that it was time for black people to share in the opportunities of state procurement, or one stood against it on the grounds that the Guptas were not proper representatives of black empowerment but merely common commercial criminals. Over time, the balance of forces shifted towards the latter side. Indeed, there are few countries in the world which have succeeded in taking a stand and fighting back against state capture. It isn't often that a country succeeds in fighting against special interests of the kind represented by the Guptas. Given how aggressive the state capture project has been, it is remarkable that the saga received the degree of exposure in the media that forced the government to accept that the problem existed. Above all, it was the heroic work of anonymous whistleblowers and investigative journalists who in some cases put their lives on the line to blow the lid off the state capture project. A whole slew of books have been published on different aspects of state capture. Among them is one by a good friend of mine, Adriaan Basson, who with co-author Pieter du Toit described the state capture beast in their book *Enemy of the People* (2017).[113] Jacques Pauw's celebrated investigative book *The President's Keepers* (2017)[114] became an instant bestseller and his launches even turned into public expressions of opposition to and denunciation of the Zuma–Gupta nexus.

In this age of aggressive public relations manoeuvres by govern-

---

113 A. Basson and P. du Toit, *Enemy of the People*. Cape Town: Jonathan Ball, 2017.
114 J. Pauw, *The President's Keepers*. Cape Town: Tafelberg, 2017.

ments and their utilisation of fake news outlets, it was a great achievement for South Africans to have successfully repelled the disinformation dished up by both the government and the Guptas, dispelled the smokescreens and acquired a fuller understanding of the complex reach of the state capture project. In an attempt to deflect public criticism, the Guptas hired the now controversial British public relations firm Bell Pottinger, who did their best to shift the public mood in the country with their campaign against "white monopoly capital". Bell Pottinger attempted to tell South Africans that their biggest enemy was not corruption by the black political elites, but the continued domination of whites in the country's economy. This strategy did not work and ultimately the British firm had to shut its doors. Although some elements of the conversation gained a life of their own, particularly the idea that something needs to be done about the predominant economic position of whites, the notion of "white monopoly capital"was revealed for what it was, a PR ruse to shelter the Gupta family.

But the most significant development in the exposure of the Guptas has been the emergence into the public sphere of the Gupta emails, the so-called GuptaLeaks, which reveal the extent of the Guptas' network and their transactions.[115] When I first heard about the existence of over two hundred thousand leaked Gupta emails, one thought came to my mind. That is, there will be very few private companies and notable individuals in the country left with any integrity when all the information contained in the emails

---

115 J. Cronje, "You can now search hundreds of #GuptaLeaks emails", *News24*, 9 November 2017. Available at: https://www.fin24.com/Economy/you-can-now-search-hundreds-of-guptaleaks-emails-20171109 (accessed 21 November 2017).

is disclosed. I have always suspected that the Gupta corruption goes much deeper than most South Africans may have thought. The emails show just how far the Gupta tentacles have reached into the heart of the country. Indeed, it is only logical that for the Guptas to have undertaken what they did, a significant part of South Africa's institutional infrastructure must have been involved in an enabling role. This includes players in government and also the private sector. In fact, soon after the emails were leaked, private companies began reeling from the disclosures, including the collapse of Bell Pottinger. Other firms whose reputations suffered were the German software company SAP[116] and the global auditing firm KPMG. In addition, it became obvious that the Guptas had also depended on help from the banks. State capture had grown beyond the specific transactions identified by the Public Protector, Advocate Thuli Madonsela, in her report of 2016.

The increasing complexity of the problem raises all kinds of difficulties. Let us picture the state capture saga in this way. Imagine running into the bush chasing after a criminal whom you have just witnessed committing a criminal act. Wearing a T-shirt with the words "Theft is us" printed on it, he is just within your reach when two hundred more people pop up and run in the same direction as the suspected criminal that you were chasing, all wearing similar "Theft is us" T-shirts. In this situation what do you do? Do you forget the one criminal you were chasing and focus on those many that have just emerged, or do you keep your eyes on the criminal

---

116 Y. Groenewald, "Why the US, not SA, critics ask SAP on state capture probe", *Fintech*, 26 October 2017. Available at: https://www.fin24.com/Tech/News/ why-the-us-and-not-sa-critics-ask-sap-on-state-capture-probe-20171026.

you were originally after, forgetting all the rest?

If we currently know much more about state capture – that it also involves some key players in the private sector – than we did when the Public Protector released her report, then it is necessary that we do not ignore our newly acquired knowledge as part of our investigations. This would do a disservice to justice. We cannot remain interested only in rounding up the usual suspects, while leaving untouched those who provided the necessary institutional infrastructure for the crime to be committed.

Reading the public mood in the wake of the exposure of ethical holes in the private sector, then president Zuma decided to set the terms of reference of the government commission into state capture, which the Public Protector had recommended, to include an investigation into corruption in the private sector, in addition to the specific terms set out in the Public Protector's report. Zuma did so not because he genuinely believed that corruption in the public sector ought to be uprooted, but simply because he wanted the inquiry to be so wide that it would dilute the specific role of his family and the Gupta family. This was a masterstroke on Zuma's part.

Although Zuma is not a friend of the anti-corruption lobby, his terms of reference are more acceptable to a broader movement which seeks to address the roots of the problem. To ignore the complicity of the private sector would lay one open to the charge that one is protecting the sector from an inquiry simply because it is too big, important and morally upright to be brought to account. This must be a consideration for President Ramaphosa, himself a successful businessman, who must avoid being seen as unduly protecting the private sector. Ramaphosa's relationship with the private sector in the country readily lends itself to interpretations that may undermine his credibility. This is one of the unintended consequences of how state capture unfolded in the country.

Up to this point, there is no indication that Ramaphosa is in any way involved in state capture. Because his hands are seen to be clean, he had a viable political platform upon which to challenge Zuma. The complexity of the issue has nevertheless forced Ramaphosa into a position where he is constantly caught between, on the one hand, those denialists of state capture in his own party who believe that if there is to be any investigation, then everyone in the country has to be investigated, and, on the other hand, those who believe that the private sector should not have to answer to any state capture charge, as it is all about Zuma and the Guptas. As the commission of inquiry into state capture proceeds, everyone is vying to influence the commission in one or other of these directions. There are those who are coming forward to testify how their ancestors suffered state capture in the past, and there are also those who say it was only the Guptas who were involved. And then there is Ramaphosa, standing in the middle of this, trying to make sense of the issues and deciding which view he should adopt in the public discourse as he takes a position on the matter.

The state capture inquiry has cast its net wider than the Guptas. This has the potential to shield the ANC as the investigations will very likely arrive at the conclusion that the problem is structural, with the ANC being a small player in the complex system of a modern liberal democracy. If the inquiry pursues a narrow focus, directed strictly at the Guptas, its findings will be criticised for making victims of a few ANC senior members, including Zuma, while leaving the perpetrators in the private sector to walk away scot-free. One thing is certain, and that is that there is no way to carry out the inquiry without putting the ANC on trial. As for Ramaphosa, he can distance himself from the sorry saga and thus avoid being put on trial together with the ANC. But his consequent failure to defend the ANC will result in his being seen as a traitor by party members. Once the full inquiry into state capture is completed, the ANC is bound to experience the aftershocks. Those will be more dangerous than the revelations of capture, and may well turn the country against the party.

11.

Ramaphosa's Worldview

—◦◦◦—

Is Ramaphosa an internationalist? It would seem so, judging from the fact that the first indication he gave of how he would take things forward in South Africa after being elected president of the ANC was announced at the meeting of the World Economic Forum in Davos, Switzerland.[117] Even before he could address South Africans back at home about his plans for the country and what was to be done about Jacob Zuma, then still the incumbent president, Ramaphosa was already making significant commitments and promises to the international community. Speaking to the media in Davos about Zuma's future, Ramaphosa told the reputable

---

117 J. Brown and L. Malope, "Ramaphosa wows Davos money", *Fin24*, 28 January 2018. Available at: https://www.fin24.com/Economy/South-Africa/ramaphosa-wows-davos-money-20180128-2 (accessed 10 February 2018).

international news outlet *Bloomberg News* that "we have taken a view that this is a very, very difficult matter".[118] Ramaphosa further promised that the wheels of change in South Africa would begin to speed up.

Prior to Davos, the only time Ramaphosa had come close to addressing the nation since his victory at Nasrec was when he delivered the annual January 8th ANC Statement. This was, however, not as president of the country, but as president of the ANC. As such, he could not be held by the nation to the promises made in a statement that was meant for the party.

Thus, the first time Ramaphosa informed South Africans that he was indeed negotiating Zuma's exit from power was on the international finance platform of the World Economic Forum. Perhaps this was not strategically planned at all and perhaps it has no bearing on how Ramaphosa wishes to relate to the international community. But whether planned or unplanned, there is an undeniable symbolism in the fact that in order to restore the confidence of the international community in South Africa's future, Ramaphosa had to use whatever available international platform to plead his case.

As far as the international media is concerned, Ramaphosa's campaign to assume charge of the ANC and of the country was an indication of the potential that his leadership promises. His ticket of

---

118 "Ramaphosa speaks Zuma exit and corruption at Davos", *Bloomberg News*, 24 January 2018. Available at: https://businesstech.co.za/news/government/221020/ramaphosa-speaks-zuma-exit-and-corruption-at-davos/ (accessed 10 February 2018).

integrity and his understanding of the need to protect the market from undue political upheaval were some of the positive aspects of his campaign that were widely reported by the reputable international media. His was seen as a presidency that was expected to draw South Africa closer once again to the international community, particularly when it comes to economic policy.

Moreover, Ramaphosa's increasing stand against state capture in South Africa was welcomed overseas and both drew on and evoked international solidarity against corruption. Following an intervention by the South African-born Labour peer Peter Hain, the British PR firm Bell Pottinger, which had been retained by the Gupta family, came in for condemnation by the British Parliament. At the same time, Hain was supportive of the Democratic Alliance's formal complaint to the UK's Public Relations and Communications Association about Bell Pottinger's involvement with the Gupta family,[119] which the DA argued had given rise to racial tensions in South Africa. In the United States, the FBI was reported to be investigating some suspected transactions involving members of the Gupta family living in the US.[120] What became apparent was that Western countries believed that Ramaphosa's stance on the issue of state capture, in addition to his business

---

119 "DA lodges complaint against Bell Pottinger over 'racial division'", *Fin24*, 2 July 2017. Available at: https://www.fin24.com/Economy/da-lodges-complaint-against-bell-pottinger-over-racial-division-20170702 (accessed 20 February 2018).

120 N. Goba, "Don't let FBI beat us to state capture probe, says Cyril", *Herald-Live*, 23 October 2017. Available at: http://www.heraldlive.co.za/politics/2017/10/23/dont-let-fbi-beat-us-state-capture-probe-says-cyril/ (accessed 10 March 2018).

relations with US- and UK-based multinational companies such as McDonald's and Lonmin, made him a natural ally of the West.

By contrast, Western powers had not enjoyed a close relationship with Zuma at all. Zuma preferred the BRICS camp (Brazil, Russia, India and China) far above Washington and London. Throughout his presidency, Zuma believed that the Western powers were conspiring to remove him. He flaunted his relationship with Russia and China to both London and Washington. During his presidency, the ANC's fascination with the idea of China as a model developmental state also gained greater ground. The burgeoning attraction and presence of China in Africa in general and South Africa in particular became of concern to Western powers. Moreover, it has been revealed that the Chinese firm China South Rail paid kickbacks to Gupta front companies on a lucrative deal to supply locomotives for the South African state-owned freight company, Transnet.[121] And before leaving office, Zuma was about to mortgage South Africa's future energy requirements to the Russians by signing a nuclear deal. While some Western companies, such as McKinsey and SAP, also participated in and benefited from state capture, they probably acted without the knowledge of their governments. The same cannot be said about the Chinese and Russian companies. Now, with Zuma gone, Ramaphosa's presidency offers the West an opportunity to displace China and even Russia in South Africa.

Unlike ANC leaders – such as Zuma – who came from the exile

---

121 "#GuptaLeaks: The great train robbery – Part 1: The Zurich tryst", *News24*, 8 March 2018. Available at: https://www.news24.com/SouthAfrica/News/ guptaleaks-the-great-train-robbery-part-1-the-zurich-tryst-20180308 (accessed 10 March 2018).

tradition, Ramaphosa is not likely to consider rewarding Russia or China for their historical solidarity with the ANC struggle against apartheid. This particular part of the history of the Cold War probably does not have a special place in Ramaphosa's political memory. He will more likely be interested in pursuing economically beneficial relations with the West, especially as his campaign for the presidency of the ANC also included a determination to revitalise the South African economy and restore economic stability. He did not say anything about securing South Africa's self-determination or sovereignty amid the competing global powers, a narrative that lies at the heart of both Russian and Chinese foreign policy.

Moreover, things have changed in the world, for China and Russia too. The Cold War is no longer in existence, at least not in the form it took prior to 1990. Russia and China are now both market societies, albeit with the state exercising a strong hand in regulating the economy. This means that the two countries will pursue their own economic interests in their dealings with Ramaphosa's presidency. They will not hold Ramaphosa to historical obligations that South Africa once might have owed to the Soviet Union or Communist China. What is more, the future of the BRICS project, which Zuma touted all over the place, is now uncertain under Ramaphosa.

It is my belief that the Russians may very well renew their efforts to build a relationship with the Ramaphosa-led government. This is partly because, of all the historical allies of the ANC, the Russians have not received due reward for their historical role in supporting the ANC's armed struggle against apartheid. Indeed, since the collapse of apartheid and the inauguration of democracy in South Africa, the Russians have made no significant economic gain from having helped the ANC. The first mega project undertaken by the ANC in a democratic South Africa, the controversial arms deal, which was mired in corruption and ended in a discredited commission of inquiry, benefited Western countries such as the UK, Sweden and Germany most of all. The Russians, for their part, did not secure any of the lucrative arms procurement contracts or get to share in any of the loot. The closest the Russians came to earning a consolation price for its historical role of support for the ANC was the preliminary steps towards a nuclear deal with Zuma. Given Ramaphosa's anti-corruption stance, it is likely that he will stay well away from such mega projects in future. If that is so, I expect that during Ramaphosa's presidency, there will be renewed efforts by the Russians to get what is historically their due. At the same time, they will have to change their tack, as they will be dealing with someone who is demonstrably not anti-West. Moreover, Ramaphosa has apparently not had any experience of the Russian way of doing things, in the way that most ANC members learned while in exile.

All in all, there will be intense competition for Ramaphosa's ear by the global community. Hence it is important for him to formulate a cogent foreign policy so as to be able to navigate between competing foreign interests. It is important for the new president to adopt clear criteria for saying yea or nay to advances made by other powers, particularly Russia, China and the United States.

At the same time, Ramaphosa's leadership offers the potential for South Africa to regain its international standing and credibility, which it lost during the Zuma era because of corruption and the decline of the ANC's legitimacy. Conditions are in general favourable for him. He has been given a clean slate to write his diplomatic and political story. What he needs to do now is to communicate his worldview and justify why it is in the interests of South Africa as a nation. If he has no pressing agenda beyond serving South Africa's interests, Ramaphosa should not choose between the West, on the one hand, and China and Russia, on the other. He has to focus on developing some coherent criteria for dealing with those countries, based on the principles that are enshrined in the South African Constitution – particularly those of human rights and human dignity. These are values that should not be traded for immediate economic gain or as an appeasement to maintain friendship with powerful countries. At the same time, the criteria should also strive to always maximise South Africa's national interests, including economic prosperity for the country as a whole. This ought in any case to be the driving force behind South Africa's foreign relations.

12.

The Private Sector

———∿———

Since the collapse of apartheid and the inauguration of a constitutional democracy, the role of the private sector in democratic consolidation in South Africa has been the proverbial elephant in the room. After Nelson Mandela's glorious presidency, Thabo Mbeki took the fight directly to the private sector, which he often accused of failing to show commitment to the new black-led dispensation. Mbeki's criticism of the private sector was couched in both Marxist class jargon and a nationalistic narrative. His African Renaissance[122] project invoked an African identity as a rallying point for self-determination in a world that did not recognise the African

---

122 A. Adebayo, "Mbeki's dream of Africa's renaissance belied South Africa's schizophrenia", *The Conversation*, 24 April 2017. Available at: https://theconversation.com/mbekis-dream-of-africas-renaissance-belied-south-africas-schizophrenia-58311 (accessed 8 March 2018).

way of life and human values. For Mbeki, the call for transformation in the private sector was a call for it to also reflect African values and embrace the talents and contributions of Africans.

When Jacob Zuma became president of the country in 2009, there were expectations that his presidency would de-escalate the tensions that had built up between the private sector and the new African political elite. Zuma's "man of the people" demeanour had earlier been interpreted to mean that he would be more consultative in his approach. However, Zuma became a problem for the private sector, not because he had, like Mbeki, an ideological bent against private enterprise, but because he began to attack it in order to deflect attention from his troubled leadership and its accumulating series of blunders and the increasing revelations of his corrupt practices. It was under Zuma that talk of "radical economic transformation"[123] gained momentum. These are policies that essentially propagate state intervention in the economy in ways that do not necessarily take into consideration the likely reaction of the markets.

Zuma had no prior commitment to anything that resembled radical economic transformation, but he used it as a mantra to explain away the concerns that the private sector had shown towards his administration, particularly about issues of corruption. As much as radical economic transformation is a genuine concern arising from the fact of growing inequality in the country, Zuma

---

123 P. Herman, "Radical economic transformation arose from ANC: Zuma", *News24*, 9 November 2017. Available at https://www.news24.com/South-Africa/News/radical-economic-transformation-arose-from-the-anc-zuma-20171109 (accessed 10 January 2018).

exploited it for the sole purpose of punishing the private sector for casting aspersions on his leadership and integrity. The incessant call by the private sector and its allies in civil society for Zuma to leave office from the time his second term started in 2014 only intensified his determination to advocate policies that were meant to be punitive towards the private sector. In this regard Zuma succeeded, in the sense that he was able to push the ANC to adopt a policy of "radical economic transformation" at the party's 54th national conference held in December 2017.

One of the policies that the ANC at the conference resolved to undertake was expropriation of land without compensation.[124] This came in response to widespread disappointment with the slow pace of land restitution in post-apartheid South Africa. Expropriation of land without compensation has the potential to have a serious effect upon food security as well as the property market in the country. Responding to the decision by Parliament in February 2018 to adopt an EFF-sponsored motion on expropriation of land without compensation, the major banks have stated that the policy could result in the collapse of some financial institutions.[125] In addition to this controversial policy, Zuma took the whole country by surprise when he announced the provision of fee-free tertiary educa-

---

124 L. Malope, "ANC decides on expropriation of land without compensation", *City Press*, 21 December 2017. Available at: https://city-press.news24.com/Special-Report/ANC_Conference/anc-decides-on-expropriation-of-land-without-compensation-20171221 (accessed 7 January 2018).

125 T. Mongoai, "Banks warn against expropriation of land without compensation", *SABCNewsOnline*, 6 March 2018. http://www.sabcnews.com/sabc-news/banks-warn-land-expropriation-without-compensation/ (accessed 9 March 2018).

tion,[126] a policy position that cannot be abandoned now that Zuma has stepped down. The provision of free tertiary education in public institutions has serious implications for the fiscus, and consequently for the private sector. Moreover, the fear is that it will add immeasurably to the government's mounting debt. If the government pursues a higher deficit, the cost of borrowing will be higher not only for government, but also for the financial institutions in the private sector. This might well erode returns on already invested money.

These were some of Zuma's parting "gifts" to the ANC and the country. Ramaphosa now has the difficult task of managing the policies he has inherited, in addition to dealing with the endemic corruption that Zuma left behind. The sad part of this story is that Zuma was probably not even really committed to radical policies, but was simply irked by the private sector and the manner in which it sought to attack his leadership. So, in the longer view, instead of reducing the tensions between the private sector and the ruling elites, Zuma's tenure institutionalised these tensions by pushing the party to adopt policy resolutions whose implementation will rattle the private sector and disrupt the logic of capitalism. What started as a personal squabble between Zuma and the private sector has been elevated to an ideological position that cannot be simply wished away even after Zuma's departure.

Where does Ramaphosa start with all this? He has to manage the crisis. This means that Ramaphosa must balance, on the one

---

126 G. Quintal, "Zuma announces free higher education", *Business Day*, 16 December 2017. Available at: https://www.businesslive.co.za/bd/national/education/2017-12-16-zuma-announces-free-higher-education/ (accessed 20 December 2017).

hand, the demands of ANC hardliners for radical economic transformation and, on the other, the expectations of the private sector
that he will bring nuance to the policy positions that have been
adopted and implement them in a way that limits the damage to
the economy. From the point of view of the private sector, Ramaphosa's presidency has been hailed as a triumph of reasonableness
when it comes to economic policies. [127]

During his campaign for the ANC presidency, Ramaphosa
held the middle line: he insisted that the ANC would indeed
implement radical economic policies but he is also understood
to favour a "sober" approach to economic transformation.[128]
What this means is that he will implement the policies in a way
that does not negatively affect food security and economic stability. This would be a reprieve to the private sector in the sense
that there are some ANC members who have resolved that these
policies will be implemented irrespective of their economic consequences.

If Ramaphosa is seen to be too concerned about the implications of the policies for the private sector, this might raise awkward
questions about his commitment to the principles that lie behind

---

127 J. Brown,"Ramaphosa's plan could boost growth to 4.5%", *City Press*, 22 April
2018. Available at: https://www.fin24.com/Economy/ramaphosas-plan-could-
boost-growth-to-45-20180422 (accessed 22 April 2018).

128 E. Naki,"Ramaphosa to take sober approach on radical economic transformation", *The Citizen*, 24 October 2017. Available at: https://citizen.co.za/news/
south-africa/1700412/ramaphosa-to-take-sober-approach-on-radical-
economic-transformation/ (accessed 2 February 2018).

ANC policies. Ramaphosa is aware of this risk, and how this might constrict his space within the ANC, and hence he has to say things like "radical economic transformation must happen urgently".[129]

If Ramaphosa can demonstrate that he is in control of the narrative regarding radical economic transformation, then he will be in a position to manage the pace and extent of the policies' implementation. To retain control of the narrative, Ramaphosa has to utter some of the populist rhetoric while at the same time relying on the nuances he can introduce to manage the impact of the policies on the economy. The private sector has to allow him to be rhetorical and populist, because that is the only way in which he can win the confidence of his comrades within the ANC and assure them that he is one of them. It is important for Ramaphosa to build trust within the ANC, to ensure that there is no strong suspicion that he might block ANC policies to secure the interests of the private sector.

Fortunately for this sector, the ANC policy resolutions have built-in disclaimers to guard against and restrict their negative consequences. Let us take, for example, the much-talked-about resolution on expropriation of land without compensation. The resolution as passed at the Nasrec conference also adds the proviso that expropriation of land without compensation should pass the "sustain-

---

129 Z. Mahlati, "#Ramaphosa: 'Radical economic transformation will happen soon'", *Independent Online*, 19 April 2017. Available at: https://www.iol.co.za/news/politics/ramaphosa-radical-economic-transformation-will-happen-soon-8729572 (accessed 20 January 2018).

ability test",[130] so as not to damage the economy or undermine food security. This condition provides Ramaphosa with leeway to manage the effects of the policy or even delay its implementation without appearing to do so. He can, for instance, commission a lengthy feasibility study on the possible impact of land expropriation on the economy. If he engages in this kind of tactic, then it becomes difficult for anyone to accuse him of abandoning the ANC policy resolution. The policy disclaimer represents Ramaphosa's victory at Nasrec.

The main problem that Ramaphosa faces in managing the situation with radical policies seems to come from the private sector, which is set on demanding what is impossible: an absolute assurance that there shall be no radical economic transformation. Some within the private sector fail to understand where the ANC find, itself after the Nasrec conference, and what space exists for Ramaphosa to manoeuvre. The use of terms like "Ramaruin" – a sentiment of disappointment expressed after the February budget speech and the VAT hike, the success of the parliamentary motion on expropriation of land without compensation, and Ramaphosa's disappointing first cabinet reshuffle[131] – shows that, for some, Ramaphosa has to make a clear, final choice between the wishes

---

130 G. Davis, "ANC to amend Constitution to allow for land expropriation without compensation", *Eyewitness News*, 20 December 2017. Available at: http://ewn.co.za/2017/12/21/anc-to-amend-constitution-to-allow-for-land-expropriation-without-compensation (accessed 6 January 2018).

131 D. Silke, "SA lurches from Ramaphoria to Ramaruin", *Fin24*, 5 March 2018. Available at: https://www.fin24.com/Opinion/sa-lurches-from-ramaphoria-to-ramaruin-20180305 (accessed 5 March 2018).

of the private sector and those of the hardliners within the ANC.

The choice for Ramaphosa, however, is not clear, because of the complexity of the situation and the current state of play between the private sector and the broader society. The private sector wants an indication that it is safe under Ramaphosa's leadership. The difficulty for Ramaphosa is that there is a cost for him if he is seen to be making too many concessions or being too yielding to the private sector. But if he achieves a good balance between the demands of the private sector and that of the broader population in the country, he stands a good chance of not compromising himself in the eyes of both sides. At the same time he will relieve himself of the burdens derived from his relations with and his own involvement in the private sector, including the burden of Marikana.

The fact is that the private sector has serious credibility issues, which have implications for Ramaphosa's leadership. If Ramaphosa does not take a firm position towards the private sector, he could find his leadership undermined by the reputational risk that the sector has incurred over the years under Zuma and before. At the same time, it would be unfair to paint the private sector as a whole with the same brush. South Africa's companies are diverse; they show different corporate cultures and relate to the government and the broader society in different ways. During the Zuma era, however, the private sector tended to coalesce and assume a common position towards Zuma's leadership for its lack of moral rectitude. In general, South African companies are likely to take a moral position only when it is convenient for them to do so.

It has become quite clear from the "GuptaLeaks" that many companies were actually involved in the state capture associated with the Gupta family. Had it not been for the complicity of South Africa's private sector in providing the institutional infrastructure for state capture, the project would not have gained such momentum. In a private conversation I had with a senior official of a major bank in South Africa, I was told that the banks knew about controversial transactions involving the Gupta family as far back as 2005. But nothing was done for a long time because the private sector originally did not see the Guptas as a threat to its businesses. Also, South Africa lacks the kind of social activism directed at the private sector that would insist on greater transparency in the way that corporates operate. Corruption in South Africa is still understood as a public sector problem, while the private sector is seen as capable of complete self-regulation.

All in all, the lesson of the Gupta saga is that South Africans should be worried about the role of the private sector in abetting corruption. If the private sector blows the whistle on corruption only when it is convenient to do so, then there are moral hazards that lie ahead for both the private sector and the broader society. This is the reason why I believe South Africa requires corporate activism to ensure that transparency and accountability within the business sector do not depend on the grace of the companies operating within it. There is a deep need for a non-punitive form of corporate activism whose focus should be to assist the private sector to play a better role in democratic South Africa. This type of activism should aim to help the corporate sector rise above its history of compliance and complicity both during the apartheid era and since then, and in particular to deal with the recent reputational issues that have engulfed businesses in the country.

For it is not only the Gupta saga that is of concern. The near collapse of the company that was once considered one of South Africa's global ambassadors, Steinhoff International Holdings, is another case in point.[132]

While Steinhoff was perfecting the art of inflating mattress sales – non-inflatable mattresses for that matter – everyone else in the private sector was fast asleep. Steinhoff had been hailed as the most successful acquisition company in recent years,[133] with its CEO Markus Jooste enjoying rock-star stature in the corporate and finance world. It is worth noting that most people in the corporate sector have not acknowledged their complicity in selling the Steinhoff success story to investors.

Steinhoff is not an isolated case. There have also been complex Ponzi schemes that have collapsed, such as Fidentia, a company that lost hundreds of millions of rands under the leadership of J. Arthur Brown as a result of his fraudulent activities.[134] Yet this scam did not inspire corporate activism in the country.

One is also reminded of Barry Tannenbaum, who was accused of running a Ponzi scheme involving the loss to investors of

132 J. Gronje, "Steinhoff files show Jooste 'repeatedly lied' to investors and regulators: PSA", *Fin24*, 26 January 2018. Available at: https://www.fin24.com/Companies/Retail/steinhoff-files-show-jooste-repeatedly-lied-to-investors-and-regulators-psa-20180126 (accessed 9 February 2018).

133 S. Harris, "Steinhoff: Is Jooste SA's top dealmaker?", *Fin24*, 29 August 2016. Available at: https://www.fin24.com/Finweek/Business-and-economy/steinhoff-is-jooste-sas-top-dealmaker-20160829 (accessed 10 February 2018).

134 M. le Cordeur, "How Fidentia fraudster stashed cash abroad: Panama leaks", *Fin24*, 4 April 2016. Available at: https://www.fin24.com/Companies/Financial-Services/how-fidentia-fraudster-stashed-cash-abroad-panama-leaks-20160404 (accessed 5 December 2017).

R12.5 billion.[135] Tannenbaum has since relocated to Australia, where he is said to be enjoying the spoils of his fraudulent activities.

Reports indicate that, in general, corporate fraud, corruption and bribery are on the rise in South Africa.[136] It is evident that the idea that private companies should be left to self-regulate is not working. At present, as the state capture saga showed, companies become complicit in economic crimes because the social costs of participating are not unbearable. What corporate activism would achieve, if activated on a wide scale, would be to increase the social cost to companies of participating in or conniving at fraud.

What is also required in this situation is political leadership with capacity to mediate the relationship between the private sector and the broader citizenry. There needs to be a proper national dialogue about the private sector in order to build a meaningful relationship between business and the broader society in which corporate social responsibility goes beyond mere public relations. Hopefully, the inquiry into state capture will provide an opportunity for citizens to renegotiate the terms of their engagement with the private sector, and at the same time demand accountability and moral rectitude from the sector. For the state capture inquiry will certainly not only investigate the public sector, but also put the private sector in South Africa on trial. For the sake of sustainability, the private sector will have to own up to its role in corruption.

135 R. Rose, "Reprieve for accused Ponzi scam lawyer", *TimesLive*, 2 May 2010. Available at: https://www.timeslive.co.za/sunday-times/business/2010-05-02-reprieve-for-accused-ponzi-scam-lawyer/ (accessed 3 January 2018).
136 PwC, "Global economic crime and fraud survey 2018", 2018. Available at: https://www.pwc.co.za/en/assets/pdf/gecs-2018.pdf (accessed 11 March 2018).

It is not yet clear whether the private sector will thrive or only survive under Ramaphosa's leadership. In Ramaphosa, the private sector may well have its man in office. However, South Africans have also reached a heightened level of awareness about the conduct of the private sector and its implications for society. It is up to Ramaphosa to help set out the conditions for his relationship with the private sector or to redefine that relationship. The private sector also has an opportunity to reinvent itself, instead of relying on political leaders to do the PR work for them. The predatory relationship between the private sector, society and political leadership needs to be reconstructed anew.

The missing link in all this is the ANC. What does the ANC expect from the private sector in future? If the ANC is interested in building a relationship with the private sector merely to extract patronage, then the problem is a bigger one. If the ANC is morally weak, as is the case now, the party's hold on government will be used to proliferate patronage. If so, the party will be vulnerable to a takeover by interest groups, including some in the private sector. As we will see in the next chapter, which looks at the challenges that exist in state-owned enterprises, the ANC, having opened the path for corruption in the public sector, will find it difficult to push for a relationship with the private sector on the basis of good governance and transparency.

13.

The State-Owned Enterprises Dilemma

———∿∿———

State-owned enterprises (SOEs), the great public utilities such as Eskom, Transnet, South African Airways and the Post Office, have been much in the public eye in recent years for all the wrong reasons: failures of governance, financial mismanagement, corruption, and involvement in state capture. Although they seem to have become self-governing behemoths, they are in fact public institutions providing essential services for the economy and the society and accountable to government ministers and state departments. Their current woes are therefore the responsibility of the government, and Cyril Ramaphosa has promised to clean them up, strengthen their governance and their financial standing, and bring their spending under control.[137] Before we consider more closely their problems

---

137 L. Omarjee, "Ramaphosa's plan for SOEs", *Fin24*, 20 February 2018. Available at: https://www.fin24.com/Economy/ramaphosas-plan-for-soes-20180220 (accessed 10 March 2018).

and proposed solutions, it is instructive to reflect briefly on their history.

The formation of public utilities was part of the industrialisation and modernisation programme that was begun and carried out by successive white governments in South Africa. Industrialisation is not only an economic project, but also a political project in which elites are typically involved. While some of the key SOEs, such as Eskom, were established by the Smuts government prior to apartheid, they acquired more shape and focus when the National Party took power in 1948 and became part of the apartheid government's burgeoning military-industrial complex. The SOEs were, in one sense, prestige national projects of the regime, showcasing the achievements of a modernising country on the make. But they also played a major role in establishing Afrikaner capital. They were "rent-extracting monopolies" that benefited the Afrikaner political and business elites.

The extraction of resources from the SOEs by the elites did not hamper the state's agenda to use the SOEs to create an industrial economy. Corruption and economic industrial development are not always mutually exclusive. The apartheid regime had it both ways. It was able to use the state-owned enterprises to build South Africa into a powerful industrial society. At the same time, the SOEs were important in implementing the National Party's agenda to tackle poverty and social deficits among its own constituents, the so-called poor whites, so as to consolidate the Afrikaner nationalist movement. Institutions such as the Post Office and the South African Railways and Harbours made a significant impact in addressing unemployment and poverty among whites during the twentieth century.

Revelations of state looting during the apartheid years have been forthcoming in recent years. Hennie van Vuuren, in his book *Apartheid, Guns and Money: A Tale of Profit* (2017), shows how state resources under apartheid were channelled towards private companies aligned with the regime. There has never been a full probe into corruption and theft of public resources under apartheid. Such an inquiry will most likely never happen. Although South Africa is currently confronting revelations of widespread looting of state-owned enterprises by business elites with political connections, there has been little reflection on the history of the problems associated with the SOEs. We have to begin with an acknowledgement that state-owned enterprises in South Africa are inherently susceptible to corruption or capture. No institutional tinkering with their structures will ever completely insulate them from such malign influences.

When the SOEs were subjected to political influence and corruption under apartheid, the state then had more capacity to ensure that the SOEs delivered on their core mandate of contributing to the building of an industrial economy. With the current challenges that have been experienced in the SOEs, the government's capacity to utilise the entities to further its policy agenda has shrunk significantly. Again, this shows that corruption is more corrosive of democratic societies than it is of repressive regimes. By their very nature, repressive regimes do not have to live up to high standards of public justification in policy making and implementation. Furthermore, the strong arm of the repressive state also ensures that tight control is exercised over the business elites who operate in the same inner circles as the ruling politicians. This means that there are fewer people who can access resources through political connections. In such regimes, corruption is centralised in a similar manner to the way power is centralised.

In post-apartheid South Africa, however, although the ANC dominates all spheres of government, there are autonomous power-brokers within the party over whom the party has been losing control. The danger is that the spread of corruption will involve more players operating in different autonomous spheres. This means that corruption could become democratised in the sense that everyone within the system who believes they are entitled to ill-gotten gains has a good chance of succeeding in stealing public funds.

What has happened to the SOEs under former president Zuma's administration is something that is in part attributable to the ANC itself. I am referring here to the investment company Chancellor House,[138] which the ANC started in the early 2000s largely to fund the party's activities, particularly its election campaigns. In 2007 Eskom awarded the single biggest contract in its history, for six steam generators worth R20 billion, to a consortium including Hitachi Power Africa, which was then 25% owned by Chancellor House. When a governing party forms an investment company through which to receive tenders from state-owned enterprises, such a party will almost inevitably interfere in the process by which tenders are awarded. The creation of Chancellor House has placed the ANC government in a compromising situation. And by showing that the party could make easy money, the ANC provided a

---

138 F. Wild, "Chancellor House made 5000% return on Hitachi deal", *Fin24*, 5 October 2015. Available at: https://www.fin24.com/Economy/Chancellor-House-made-5-000-return-on-Hitachi-deal-20151005 (accessed 10 December 2017).

blueprint for state capture. It was also in effect inviting other groups and individuals to participate and compete with the party in this enterprise of self-enrichment. What we now have in South Africa are multiple criminal enterprises competing to steal public funds. The battle between these groups, drawn from both the political and business elites, can only hamper the development of democracy in the country and hold the society to ransom.

The dominant narrative emanating from the private sector in South Africa is that the state-owned enterprises should be privatised to ensure that they are properly run. Some believe that this would release the taxpayer from the constant burden of having to bail out the SOEs. South African Airways, for instance, is understood to exist on a permanent bail-out diet. Therefore, by privatising the airline, the company will be managed properly in line with the principles of governance found in the private sector. The problem with this solution is that it fails to take into account any moral basis for selling state assets to the private sector simply because the assets are poorly managed at the moment under public control. Besides, there is no way that a fair price could be determined for the sale of such public entities, in which the nation has invested, even through bail-outs, over many years. State assets are almost always sold for scrap, only to be subsequently revalued at a much higher price to repay the loan by which they were purchased by private individuals or companies.

The argument on the other side is that state-owned enterprises ought to remain public assets and that they should not be sold to private individuals or companies. This view holds that SOEs exist to further the government's development agenda whose implementation cannot be subordinated to the interests of private individuals. This is the idea that refuses to die in the ANC and it has undergone an interesting refinement: that SOEs are strategic not only for government's development agenda but also for the ANC's development agenda.

Retaining control of key state-owned enterprises such as Transnet and Eskom is one of the policy positions that have been doing the rounds within the ANC for a while now. With the adoption of radical economic policies including expropriation of land without compensation, it is difficult to imagine how the plan that Ramaphosa has floated of a "centralised oversight model" for the SOEs will actually work in stabilising the ailing entities.[139] By restructuring the bureaucracy through which state-owned enterprises account for their activities and finances, Ramaphosa will only have restructured the ways in which the problem expresses itself, while the problem would still remain. In other words, it will only change the way in which the symptoms of bad governance within the SOEs are expressed. The problem with SOEs is not the way in which they account, or who they account to. The problem has to do with the philosophy upon which SOEs were founded and which has evolved over the years. To change this political economy requires a different way of thinking altogether.

In order for Ramaphosa to fully restructure the SOEs, there should firstly be some realignment of the ANC's political will that

---

139   G. Davis, "Ramaphosa spells out plans for better oversight, coordination of SOEs", *Eyewitness News*, 20 February 2018. Available at: http://ewn.co.za/2018/ 02/20/ramaphosa-spells-out-plans-for-better-oversight-coordination-of- soes (accessed 11 March 2018).

would secure the release of the SOEs from the political agenda of the party. The National Party could not do this. Instead, what the National Party government did was to wield stern control over the entire government bureaucracy, including the SOEs, and in this way managed to control the patronage involving the SOEs, something that the ANC has allowed to slip out of its hands. This is where authoritarianism shows an advantage over democracy when it comes to managing corruption. Under the National Party's repressive regime, institutions such as the SOEs were never captured by interest groups whose agendas were contrary to those of the ruling elites. Under former president Zuma's administration, on the other hand, the ANC lost out because its development agenda was sidestepped by the business agenda of the Guptas and their associates within the ANC. As the ANC became negligent in implementing its development agenda, competing agendas took over at the SOEs and put an end to control by the ANC.

The only way for Ramaphosa to save the SOEs from corruption is to manage the ANC and find ways to extend his government's political agenda without having to use the SOEs as a platform. This can be achieved by rethinking the ownership model of the SOEs and also considering at the same time how this will change their vulnerability to influence by the political elites. Ramaphosa will have to ask the ANC to take its hands out of the cookie jar for once, and allow a mixed ownership model for the SOEs. In my view, a certain amount of ownership of the SOEs should be leased out to private entities for a specified period of time. Private entities should not, however, be allowed permanent ownership of the assets.

This proposed solution stands in the middle of the two extremes that have shaped discussions so far about how to reconstitute the SOEs. It would be interesting to expose the SOEs to the logic of the private sector while at the same time retaining state control to ensure that the entities are deliberately utilised to pursue the government's development agenda. There will always be conflict in balancing private interests and public interests. Resolving this problem by placing entities under the total control of the private sector would certainly not inevitably or necessarily ensure that the development agenda which the country needs will be advanced. This is not to say that the private sector cannot be trusted to pursue the nation's development. However, it should not be the role of the private sector to concern itself primarily with that responsibility.

Centralising control of the SOEs, as Ramaphosa proposes, either under a commission or the Department of Public Enterprises will bring about further challenges, perhaps even greater challenges than what has been experienced before. For one thing, a centralised structure creates a single-point failure system. The reason why there has thus far been such a positive response to the idea of centralising control of the SOEs is not that this is an institutionally sound and structurally superior means of addressing the problem. For instance, critical questions have yet to be raised as to how the idea of centralised control can be reconciled with the democratic principle of a decentralised bureaucracy.

The reason why Ramaphosa's centralisation plan has not raised concerns is the widespread belief that the man is incorruptible and therefore will centrally manage crises well. If Ramaphosa were to suggest shrinking the provinces from a total of nine to only three, which he would personally manage through a cellphone app, many would wake up, after days of agreeing with him, to realise they just agreed to the very centralised management which they detested under Thabo Mbeki's administration. When a political leader seems to carry more credibility than the institutions over which he or she presides, it is then that the nation has to make sure that such credibility is not abused.

Had Zuma suggested centralising the control of SOEs and called it "streamlining", no one would have listened to him and he would surely have been accused of planning grand theft. At this point in time, however, South Africans are searching again for their messiah, and they would be willing to let go of a principle or two to find him. The country is desperate to be led. But it is important, all the same, to ensure that proper thought is given to how to rein in the SOEs. I do not believe that the ANC administration has a solid mandate to be trusted to restructure the SOEs. What it can at least do under Ramaphosa before the 2019 elections is to close the tap to ensure there is no longer wastage at the SOEs. Restructuring the SOEs is a significant project that needs to be thought about only once a mandate has been given to the party in the 2019 elections. After all that has been revealed about how state-owned enterprises were pillaged under an ANC government, it is difficult to trust the party to act in the public interest with respect to the SOEs.

For now, Ramaphosa should outline what he plans to do with the SOEs if his government is voted in in 2019. This does not mean that the president has to undertake a major overhaul of the entities before the elections. His government in fact lacks a sufficient mandate to undertake such a potentially significant task as this. The political mandate given to the ANC in the 2014 general

elections has now expired. What Ramaphosa can do in the meantime is strengthen his hand by reducing corruption in the state-
owned enterprises. This is not a big project; all it takes is firing and
hiring. As for a major overhaul of the SOEs, it is important for
Ramaphosa to take his time and wait for an appropriate mandate
at the elections in 2019.

14.

Divide and Rule

———≈≈≈———

Never before in recent years have we witnessed opposition parties in South Africa struggling as much as now to decide on how to deal with an ANC president. The initial optimism, or "Ramaphoria", that society seems to have shown towards Cyril Ramaphosa's new presidency has had the opposition taking a mild "wait-and-see" approach: let's wait for him to be dragged down by the ANC and then we will continue attacking the party.

The opposition's response to Ramaphosa's presidency thus far has not advanced much beyond the way it related to him during his presidential campaign. When Ramaphosa first began to speak up against former president Jacob Zuma, the opposition saw fit to support him simply because he made himself available as a pawn in their fight against Zuma. As Zuma's disastrous tenure was slowly winding down throughout 2017, the opposition parties joined forces in inaugurating Ramaphosa as the president even before his election in early 2018. They accepted him as a man of reason. In one parliamentary question session while he was still deputy to Zuma, some DA members of Parliament even referred to Ramaphosa as "Mr President".

The question that needs to be posed is whether it was strategic of the opposition parties to warm up to Ramaphosa in this way, locating him as it were outside the ANC. Perhaps their attitude towards him was a reflection of South Africans' desperation to find someone positive to reflect political developments in the country. Even the EFF toned down its attacks on Ramaphosa in public, often promising to support him on condition that he acted outside the parameters of the ANC as a political party. EFF leader Julius Malema went as far as predicting in public that Ramaphosa would win the contest to lead the ANC. Malema reportedly said that he did not believe Nkosazana Dlamini-Zuma stood a chance against Ramaphosa.[140] If we look at what happened at Nasrec, Malema was not entirely correct in assuming Dlamini-Zuma stood no chance. As explained earlier, Ramaphosa won the leadership battle with the help and political support of the controversial David Mabuza. Had Mabuza decided not to betray the Zuma faction and abandon its candidate, chances are that Dlamini-Zuma could have won the contest. This seems to be confirmed by the slim margin between the votes Dlamini-Zuma and Ramaphosa eventually received.

---

140 "Cyril will lead ANC, says Malema", *TimesLive*, 15 December 2017. Available at: https://www.timeslive.co.za/politics/2017-12-15-cyril-will-lead-anc-says--malema/ (accessed 20 February 2018).

In the period leading up to the elective conference at Nasrec, the two big opposition parties in South Africa took a public position on the internal leadership succession squabble within the ANC, and openly supported Ramaphosa against the incumbent president's well-publicised wish that Dlamini-Zuma would succeed him. It seems the opposition parties were smitten by Ramaphosa, just as the private sector had been. Of course, the opposition also made cautionary noises. But the caution was not about Ramaphosa as an individual; it was about his leadership of a party engrossed in its own internal politics and factional battles.

For a moment, just when it became clear that Ramaphosa was going to become the president of the country after he won the ANC leadership contest, it almost looked as if the opposition parties were about to close up shop and call it a day. Having to quickly shift gear from the Zuma presidency to Ramaphosa, the opposition parties have since allowed their political cooperation to disintegrate. For example, the DA and the EFF have not even shared a stage since Ramaphosa was inaugurated as president of the country in February 2018.

Before Ramaphosa took over, opposition parties often agreed on political issues, especially when it came to their opposition against Zuma, corruption and state capture. They often formed a united front against the ANC and worked together when they agreed on issues. They even shared press conferences to explain how they would deal with Zuma's transgressions. Under Zuma, these parties were clearly united in their views of what their role should be.

The Nkandla court ruling, in which Zuma was found to have failed to protect the Constitution, was the outcome of an application brought by the EFF, the UDM and the Congress of the People (COPE), who were joined by the DA.[141] The opposition parties were also united in their response to the court ruling that Parliament should initiate a process for impeaching Zuma.[142] The last grand agreement among the opposition parties occurred with their response to the court's decision that Zuma's appointment of Shaun Abrahams as head of the National Prosecuting Authority should be set aside.[143] In this case, not only did the opposition parties agree among themselves, but they also approved of the court's suggestion that Ramaphosa, as deputy president, should appoint the new prosecution head to replace Abrahams. Those were the days of the "concurrence roundtable",[144] when the opposition parties just could not agree more with each other. At times the opposition parties even shared legal counsel in some of the cases they brought to court.

Things were going so well during that time that the DA and the EFF cobbled together "pay-as-you-go" coalitions to govern three big metros: the City of Johannesburg, Nelson Mandela Bay (Port

141 K. Patel, "ConCourt: Parliament has failed to hold Zuma to account", *Mail & Guardian*, 29 December 2017. Available at: https://mg.co.za/article/2017-12-29-concourt-parliament-has-failed-to-hold-zuma-to-account (accessed 13 March 2018).

142 K. Child, "A few things that you need to know about the Zuma impeachment case", TimesLive, 29 December 2017. Available at: https://www.timeslive.co.za/politics/2017-12-29-a-few-things-that-you-need-to-know-about-the-zuma-impeachment-case/ (accessed 14 March 2018).

143 C. Mailovoch, "Court sets aside appointment of Shaun Abrahams as prosecutions chief", *Business Day*, 8 December 2017. Available at: https://www.businesslive.co.za/bd/national/2017-12-08-court-sets-aside-appointment-of-shaun-abrahams-as-prosecutions-chief/ (accessed 14 March 2018).

144 https://www.youtube.com/watch?v=DKsxogqj35g (accessed 13 April 2018).

Elizabeth) and the City of Tshwane.[145] I call the arrangement "pay-as-you-go" because the two parties did not agree on a long-term strategy for cooperating in these metropolitan municipalities. Just as with a pay-as-you-go mobile phone arrangement, each and every time a decision has to be made in the coalition arrangement between the DA and the EFF, someone has to top up the agreement and buy airtime on the go. This is because there is no prior long-term commitment that will bind parties to agree on future decisions. The future is not bound to anyone, and the DA has learned this recently with the EFF's declared intention to pull out of the coalition in Nelson Mandela Bay[146] just to teach the DA a lesson in hand-to-mouth political arrangements.

The relationships between the opposition parties during the Zuma era were all about punishing the ANC. This proved to be a short-term goal which was easily achieved. The question is: with Zuma gone, where does this leave the opposition?

Since Ramaphosa was inaugurated, it has become clear that while the opposition camp was enjoying its short-lived unity against Zuma, individual parties were covertly plotting to upstage each other when the opportunity arose. The opposition in South Africa is made up of a conglomeration of agendas and interests that

145 "South Africa's coalitions: Here's what is happening in major metros", *Business Tech*, 15 August 2016. Available at: https://businesstech.co.za/news/general/133306/south-africas-coalitions-heres-what-is-happening-in-major-metros/ (accessed 3 December 2018).

146 K. Masweneng, "EFF flexing its muscle by threatening to remove Trollip: Analysts", *HeraldLive*, 28 February 2018. Available at: http://www.herald-live.co.za/politics/2018/02/28/eff-flexing-muscle-threatening-remove-trollip-analysts/ (accessed 13 March 2018).

cannot be reconciled into a single political project. The DA has a stronger electoral share as an opposition party, having won 22% of the votes in the 2014 general elections. The EFF is sitting at 6.4%, though it appears not to be fazed by the wide electoral margin between itself and the DA. Nor does the EFF have respect for the DA and its leader, Mmusi Maimane.[147]

The key issue that has pitted the two big opposition parties against each other since Ramaphosa took over is the question of land expropriation without compensation. After the EFF joined forces with the ANC to adopt the parliamentary motion to expropriate land without compensation, the DA was left in the cold and was forced to craft the opposition's response to the motion. This is an issue that signalled a big policy shift by the ANC under Ramaphosa. Even more fascinating, the land issue seems to signal the beginning of an era of alliance between the EFF and the ANC. Such an alliance spells trouble for the opposition, and it has revealed the fault lines in the broader opposition camp.

The problems within the opposition are not limited to the relationship between the DA and the EFF. They also affect other, smaller opposition parties such as Bantu Holomisa's United Democratic Movement (UDM) and Terror Lekota's COPE, neither of which enjoys any significant popular support. Responding to the passing of the parliamentary motion to expropriate land without

---

147 S. Shoba, "Malema and Maimane: Political opposites effective in political opposition", *Sunday Times*, 23 July 2017. Available at: https://www.timeslive. co.za/sunday-times/news/2017-07-22-malema-amp-maimane-political-opposites-effective-in-political-opposition/ (accessed 12 March 2018).

compensation, COPE vowed to go to court to challenge the implementation of what it referred to as an essentially unconstitutional policy. The DA has also indicated that the party stands against the policy,[148] and is likely to go to court too.

Thus, one thing that Ramaphosa has so far achieved is to destabilise the opposition by revealing that all it enjoyed under Zuma was a marriage of convenience, which is now falling apart. By pulling the EFF to its corner on the land issue, or perhaps moving to the EFF's corner, Ramaphosa's ANC has orchestrated a situation where opposition parties will be heading to court – not to take a stand against the ANC, but to take a stand against each other. It is a divide-and-rule strategy at its best. The EFF does not have a problem with this because the party has no commitment to strengthening opposition politics in any case. The EFF does not even have a history of committing to constitutional principles, unless in circumstances where it provides good political mileage, such as the Constitutional Court case on Nkandla. It is the goal of the EFF to dismember the Constitution so as to ensure implementation of the party's radical policies, which cannot pass the constitutional muster. For the present, the EFF will stand by the Constitution so long as that is what it takes to stage a legitimate amendment to the text. It is quite sinister for a political party to adhere to the principle of constitutionalism and constitutional supremacy only for the purpose of effecting a legitimate constitutional amendment.

---

148 C. Manyathela, "DA to challenge to challenge land expropriation with every tool available", *Eyewitness News*, 12 March 2018. Available at: http://ewn.co.za/2018/03/12/da-to-challenge-land-expropriation-with-every-tool-available (accessed 12 March 2018).

The ultimate goal here is not to protect the Constitution, but to remove constitutional hurdles in the pursuit of an agenda. The ANC is also setting itself up for this route, and the DA is isolated in pushing back against this move.

This prompts the question: what exactly is the meaning of constitutionalism among the opposition parties in South Africa? The idea of constitutionalism entails "limited government",[149] in which the power of the majority is constantly kept under constitutional surveillance. While the opposition ganged together to defend the Constitution against Zuma's relentless attacks, not all parties who joined in on this appreciate the principle of constitutionalism. Building a constitutional state and instilling the idea of constitutional supremacy is not the concern, for instance, of the EFF. What the EFF seeks to achieve in its brand of opposition is to build a culture of constitutional amendment in line with the will of the majority. Yet, unlike ordinary laws, the Constitution should not be amended simply because it poses hurdles to a particular political project. Constitutional amendment should not be resorted to in the course of normal political engagements.

There is interesting literature in comparative judicial studies focusing on the concept of "unconstitutional constitutional amendments".[150] This is not an area where the EFF is afraid to tread. Anyone can guess how the EFF will most likely respond if the

---

149 K.K. Mohau,"Constitutionalism and constitutional amendment in Lesotho: A case for substantive limitation", *Lesotho Law Journal*, 21, 1, 2014.

150 R. Dixon,"Transnational constitutionalism and unconstitutional constitutional amendments", Chicago Public Law and Legal Theory Workshop, Working Paper no. 394, 2011.

Constitutional Court declares some constitutional amendments unconstitutional, either procedurally or substantively. It will most likely rebuke the court. When Chief Justice Mogoeng Mogoeng dissented in a case involving the impeachment of Zuma, the EFF did not waste time in rebuking Mogoeng.[151] Although the dissenting judgment was seen a spoiler opinion by the chief justice, Mogoeng's intention in my view was to restrain public sentiments that wanted to see Zuma impeached even if there was no discernible constitutional provision for this. The principle of constitutionalism requires this kind of restraint on the majority even when the majority appears to be right.

Now that the ANC has teamed up with the EFF to implement some radical policies in a manner that may not be constitutional, the DA has been left on its own and could easily be seen to be pursuing a form of anti-majoritarian politics. With the opposition destabilised and the ANC's project of frustrating the opposition under way, the DA cannot win this fight on its own.

What this shows is that the opposition parties were earlier not united by a basic understanding of constitutionalism, but worked together on the basis of political convenience. The uniting force behind that cooperation has since disappeared when Zuma left office. The opposition now has to start afresh and construct a new strategy of opposition politics. I personally do not think that there

---

151 K. Child, "EFF slams chief justice for interrupting fellow judge", *TimesLive*, 29 December 2017. Available at: https://www.timeslive.co.za/politics/2017-12-29-eff-slams-chief-justice-for-interrupting-fellow-judge/ (accessed 13 March 2018).

is sufficient time before the 2019 elections for the opposition to achieve this mammoth task, especially as the ANC is hell-bent on dividing the opposition by reaching out to the EFF.

When it comes to competitive electoral politics, unity among political competitors is not always good for the nation. Unity might be good for electoral victory, but it is bad for the quality of political life experienced by the nation. When the ANC and the EFF unite to implement policies in a potentially unconstitutional manner, what suffers is the principle of constitutionalism. Any restraints on the majority from unduly dominating the political space also go by the way. There will be no stable democracy if the majority do as they wish without having to worry about minorities or even those who disagree with them.

There is no denying the fact that the EFF has been a very significant part of opposition politics in South Africa since the party entered Parliament in 2014. The problem is that the EFF does not believe in the idea of the opposition as an essential part of politics. It sees opposition as important only because it believed the ANC as a party was in the wrong hands after Zuma took over. It is one thing to believe in opposing the ANC because of personal problems within the ANC. It is quite another to play a role as an opposition party in the belief that democracy is strengthened through having a strong opposition.

What is the destiny of the EFF in South African politics? Is it to build a strong brand of opposition or to ultimately return to the ANC once the rifts between them are healed? With Zuma gone and Ramaphosa now president of the ANC, rumours of a possible return of the EFF to the ANC refuse to die down. Even struggle stalwart Winnie Mandela, shortly before her death, stated her wish for Malema to return to the ANC.[152] This statement on its own has the potential to sow mistrust within the opposition and also within the EFF. By calling upon Malema to return to the ANC, ANC leaders are showing that they do not recognise the great deal of work that Malema and the EFF have achieved in the opposition since his expulsion from the party. Even worse, the call for Malema to return is a failure by the ANC to acknowledge the severity of the problems that engulfed the party under Zuma.

In the unlikely event that Malema is flattered and returns to the ANC, this will allow the ANC simply to walk away from the Zuma problems without having to take responsibility for them. Besides, there are senior EFF leaders who will not return to the ANC because they have found their space in opposition. If Malema abandons the EFF, the EFF will most likely continue to exist, perhaps even in a better form because the new EFF would evolve away from the personal-squabble style of opposition that Malema imposed on it. Furthermore, the EFF might even evolve away from Malema's authoritarian style of leadership. The EFF needs to strongly repudiate the call by the ANC to return.

Collaboration between the EFF and the ANC on the issue of expropriation of land has the potential to reduce the electoral support that the DA attained in the 2014 elections. The ANC is set on managing the EFF, to the detriment of opposition politics in the country. This could either harm the DA severely if the party does

---

152 "There is 'zero chance' for Malema to return back to ANC, Mpofu", *SABC*, 12 March 2018. Available at: http://www.sabcnews.com/sabcnews/zero-chance-malema-back-anc-mpofu/ (accessed 13 March 2018).

not formulate a cogent response, or it could actually relieve the DA from the need to compete with the EFF for opposition space. If the DA bites the bullet and confronts the EFF and the ANC on the land issue, the DA would in turn show that it is not engaged in a gentleman's agreement type of opposition politics, but rather in pursuing principled opposition politics. There is always a price to pay for assuming a principled position in politics. The question is whether the DA is willing to pay the price in the short term of distancing itself from the EFF and then reformulating opposition politics while the EFF is enjoying being flattered by the ANC.

The price tag that will come the DA's way if the party distances itself from the EFF is the loss of key metros in Johannesburg, Tshwane and Nelson Mandela Bay. In early 2018 the EFF, then in a ruling coalition with the DA in Nelson Mandela Bay metro, warned that the party would remove the DA mayor, Athol Trollip – efforts that will fail as long as smaller opposition parties in the council continue to side with the DA. The reason Malema offered was that Trollip "is white".[153] As far as I can remember, Trollip has been white as far back as the day the EFF decided to enter into an informal coalition with Trollip's party after the 2016 local government elections. If the DA accepts the mayor's removal in Nelson Mandela Bay Metro and retains the coalition in Johannesburg and Tshwane, it is only a matter of time before Malema starts denouncing the two DA mayors in the other municipalities as Uncle Toms. In my view, the DA should rather release itself from the EFF coali-

---

153 N. Gous, "EFF want to remove Trollip because he's white", *TimesLive*, 4 March 2018. Available at: https://www.timeslive.co.za/politics/2018-03-04-eff-wants-to-remove-trollip-because-hes-white/ (accessed 13 March 2018).

tion because the conditions that govern those coalitions will tear the party apart eventually. The DA should rather deal with this problem now and pay the price.

The only political party that seems to be gaining from the informal coalitions between the DA and the EFF is the ANC. Some DA members certainly have a problem voting for a party that gets into bed with the EFF for the sake of political convenience. The EFF also bears a cost from its cooperation with the DA. It comes across as being the great unprincipled operator in South African politics: a party that would get into an agreement with anyone irrespective of major policy differences. The EFF comes out of this arrangement as the disruptor and not necessarily the implementer of a sustainable, long-term political programme. All this must be pleasing to the ANC.

For the ANC, what is better than a coalition between opposition parties that can hardly agree on anything? The net effect of the coalitions for the ANC is that the opposition parties engage in squabbles that reduce their attraction to the voting public. I have argued before that opposition parties in South Africa are still miles away from coalescing on policy positions. Indeed, the opposition should not try to cobble together unworkable coalitions whose maintenance is too burdensome for the long-term stability of opposition politics in the country. More groundwork needs to be done by opposition parties before they enter into coalitions to govern. If coalitions are not thought through deeply beforehand, they will pose a threat to the growth and stability of the opposition. This is already happening to the DA.

I have had discussions with a senior DA politician who told me that the EFF has been demanding that party cadres be deployed to high-paying positions in the City of Johannesburg. The motive is not entirely a corrupt one. I hear that the EFF wants those positions so that the party can have access to money to fund some of the party's activities. This demand, I was told, came when the EFF realised that it has thus far not secured adequate returns from the coalition with the DA in the municipality. The EFF had earlier refused key appointments so as not to be seen by its followers as completely comfortable with the DA. Now the EFF hopes that it can actually extract financial resources for the party from the coalition with the DA. I have no indication whether the DA agreed to this proposal. However, it is important to ask how this differs from the way in which the ANC has allegedly used its hold on government to secure financial gains to fund party activities. Gaining financial returns from coalitions is not a principled condition for maintaining such agreements. Perhaps if the DA-led municipality in Nelson Mandela Bay offers the EFF key appointments there, the EFF will start seeing Trollip as less white. This is a condition that the DA will find it difficult to meet as time goes on. It's like trying to pay off a loan shark. The interest rate is so severe that the principal amount will never be paid up.

Among the issues upon which South Africans will cast their vote in 2019 will be the coherence of the opposition politics and the ability of opposition parties to sustain political projects. The enthusiastic response of parties such as the DA to Ramaphosa's victory might overshadow the progress they have made in earning respect for the opposition they mounted against Zuma.

There is not sufficient time for the opposition parties to reinvent themselves before the 2019 elections. Starting from now, the opposition has to learn to consider Ramaphosa as an ANC leader, to a great extent controlled by the ANC collective, instead of a lone ranger with expectations that he can act outside his party and do as he pleases. The challenges faced by the opposition also stem from the opposition camp itself. The DA needs to consider its relationship with the other opposition parties, including the smaller one-percenters. The DA, as the biggest opposition party in the country, should lead without dictating to the other parties. Up to now, the party has not been able to demonstrate that humility.

As for the EFF, it has an uncertain future in opposition. Malema seems to be flattered by the ANC's reaching out to him to return to the fold. Whether or not he returns, the issue is potentially divisive for the EFF. The EFF has to decide whether it is an opposition party destined to return to the ANC or a party that is an opposition in its own right. Unless the opposition parties get their act together and begin to cooperate for the greater good, they may have to learn a hard lesson in the 2019 general elections.

15.

Conclusion

──〜〜──

President Ramaphosa has an almost impossible task ahead of him. On the one hand, he has to battle with his own party and, on the other, he has to ensure that he does not offend the ANC to the point that the party rejects him. He has to tread carefully, at times changing colours like a chameleon in order to fit into the prevailing circumstances. The state of the ANC is such that it needs Ramaphosa to put it back on the path of common sense. There is no question that the party suffered extensive damage in its second decade of presiding over a democratic dispensation in the country. The ANC enters the third decade of democratic governance limping. The situation requires that the ANC "self-correct", as has been widely remarked.

I do not believe, though, that political parties self-correct; the only thing they really respond to is the reality of losing elections.

In his book *An Economic Theory of Democracy* (1957), Anthony Downs argues that political parties exist purely to win elections and assume power. However, nations can set conditions under which elections are winnable for a party, presuming that elections are free and fair. These are conditions that could incline parties towards the pursuit of public interests. Parties that do not respond to what people demand do not survive. Parties sell programmes and policies, while nations decide what is worth exchanging their votes for.

The ANC's story in this regard is complicated. Although it has had a terrible decade under Zuma's presidency, the ANC has not failed entirely. Did Jacob Zuma destroy the ANC? Not completely. ANC-led governments have implemented some of the most progressive policies in the world, even under the Zuma presidency. Amid corruption and allegations of state capture, there has been a comprehensive roll-out of the world's biggest anti-HIV/AIDS programme in the form of the provision of antiretroviral medicine. Furthermore, the current social security programme in South Africa counts among the world's most comprehensive. We can disagree about whether this programme is economically sustainable or not. The fact is that at this moment about 17 million people in South Africa depend on social grants.[154] There are more people on social grants than those who are formally employed. Any sudden withdrawal of the welfare programme will create not only a social crisis,

---

154 "There are officially more South Africans on social grants than working: IRR", *Business Tech*, 21 June 2017. Available at: https://businesstech.co.za/news/business/180503/there-are-officially-more-south-africans-on-social-grants-than-people-who-work-irr/ (accessed 10 March 2018).

but also an economic one. To these remarkable achievements we can also add the provision of houses, water, electricity, and more.

However, the proliferation of corruption in the country during the Zuma years has undermined the ANC's good story. The ANC that Ramaphosa has inherited suffers from a deep crisis of legitimacy. People assess the party not only in terms of the impact and success of its policies, but also on its ability to act in the interest of the people. Just like the economy, democracy is also a game of confidence. Ramaphosa's job is thus less about inventing policies that would substantively change the lives of people and the direction of the country, and more about being seen as capable of working for the public good. It took decades for the ANC to build the moral legitimacy to lead South Africa: it took only two successive presidential terms to destroy that. The question is: can the ANC under Ramaphosa's leadership regain its historical legitimacy?

The task is certainly doable, but the conditions are not readily favourable. What I hope I have shown in this book is that Ramaphosa has to do two things in parallel within a short space of time. He has to convince the ANC that the party needs his help to regain some lost moral ground. I say "some" because not all will be retrievable. The society has developed a degree of cynicism towards political leadership and there will always be doubts about the intentions behind ANC policy positions. Not all is lost, however. Again, it will take a great deal of work and reflection to regain what has been squandered.

If the ANC rejects Ramaphosa's rescue efforts in favour of remaining inward-looking in justifying its course of action, the party will encounter serious challenges in securing a sound electoral victory in the 2019 elections, as well as thereafter. This brings me to the second task that Ramaphosa ought to carry out: he has to convince South Africans that the ANC is still worth investing their votes in. Former president Zuma once stated at a business dinner that if you invest in or donate to the ANC, the ANC will look after you. Ramaphosa will have to make a similar case, albeit to a much wider audience. He has to demonstrate to the nation that the ANC is still a bankable entity. The medium of exchange in this transaction is not money, but votes, services and trust.

The only way the broader population outside the ANC will look towards the ANC for solutions is if Ramaphosa can demonstrate that he is in charge and can indeed rehabilitate the ANC. This is a difficult task because the odds are stacked against him within his own party. There are many vultures circling him. If he stumbles and falls, he will not be given an opportunity to stand up. He will be devoured first by his own comrades within the party and then by the nation, which is suspicious of the multiple agendas that seem to be part of his presidency. Ramaphosa's presidency is the most complicated since the dawn of democracy; but so is South Africa as a society.

On the one hand, Ramaphosa has to show the ANC that he will not renege on the party's historical progressive agenda, as outlined in the Freedom Charter. He has to do this in a way that also makes the ANC an attractive party capable of managing a modern democratic society. He cannot be too nostalgic about the principles of the Freedom Charter, because that would mean he is incapable of positioning the ANC as a modern party within a globalised world. With a predominantly younger population in the country,

Ramaphosa's ANC also has to be able to respond to the historical challenges through modern means associated with a market society. Poor people have dreams too, and they also dream in modern ways, despite their problems being historical and even pre-modern in origin. At present, the ANC is experiencing problems in crafting modern solutions to historical problems. What the party seems to do is propose old solutions simply because the problems that are confronted are old. This is a matter of orientation and philosophy, but it shows a lack of creativity and adaptability on the ANC's part.

In this book I sought to answer the question whether Ramaphosa can reinvent the ANC while remaining within it. I believe the answer is yes, but not without running into serious risk of the house collapsing over his head. If that happens, Ramaphosa cannot blame Zuma for weakening the foundation of the house. The blame for the collapse of the house would lie squarely with the man who undertook the job of restoring it. This means that Ramaphosa should be very careful and incremental in his approach to rescuing the ANC. But he should also be aware that time is running out, and if he does not get the job done in time, the house will collapse in the first storm of the season. He has to learn to smile next to his controversial deputy, David Mabuza, even if they disagree on fundamental matters. So far, Ramaphosa has not been able to wear a convincing smile in difficult circumstances. When he announced the cabinet reshuffle that saw Mabuza appointed deputy president and Malusi Gigaba and Bathabile Dlamini retained in cabinet, the newly elected president's body language and facial expressions indicated distaste. Seeing the president upset while reading out the names of his cabinet from hell was good for those who wanted him to take a strong anti-corruption stance, but it could hurt his relations with his comrades in the party. A smile would have done the job.

Ramaphosa cannot win the 2019 elections without a united ANC standing fully behind him. He needs to carry the ANC with him. I myself thought it was unstrategic of him to assume the presidency before the 2019 elections. I would have suggested that he focus instead on healing the wounds of Nasrec to ensure that there is not a single branch that harbours misgivings about supporting him in 2019. I thought that by avoiding going straight to the Union Buildings after Zuma's departure from office in early 2018, Rama-phosa could have time to focus on winning over all branches of the ANC, walking the walk with them. Ramaphosa cannot dance, so he has apparently found his niche in walking. Those "health walks" he has been undertaking should be extended to the rest of the country. Ramaphosa should walk with villagers, township residents, farm workers, taxi drivers and even miners right round the country. This would help in ensuring he has the ANC with him in 2019.

An ANC electoral victory in 2019 does not on its own guarantee that Ramaphosa will have a smooth sailing in convincing the ANC to implement sound policies. Whether or not the ANC will fully implement the radical economic policies adopted at the Nasrec conference is uncertain. It could be that the ANC is only con-cerned to give lip service to those policies, with a view to manag-ing the EFF and retaining some control over the rhetoric of the progressive agenda in the country. There are people such as Max du Preez[155] who have said that Ramaphosa agreed to the EFF's motion of expropriation of land without compensation not because he genuinely believes it is a good thing to do, but merely to manage the EFF's ambition to position itself as the only champion of radical policies in the country. It is difficult to tell a man's intentions when he is so deliberately cagey about them.

I am of the view that the margin of victory for the ANC in the 2019 elections will determine the extent and pace of implementation of radical economic policies in an interesting manner. In a sense, the strength that the ANC will feel itself to possess after the elections will determine the space for Ramaphosa to manoeuvre. If the ANC wins 2019 by a large majority, let's say over 60%, the party will feel strong enough to go ahead and experiment with radical economic policies. But a strong ANC could become arrogant and believe it does not need Ramaphosa to assist it further or help it mend its relationship with the broader society. Ramaphosa will have to stand by and observe as the party implements what it will believe to be a well-earned mandate. This is the worst-case scenario for Ramaphosa and the country. The party will again simply write off Zuma's wrongdoing as a misdemeanour, as it did when it protected him for so many years during his presidency. There would also be no further reason for the party to reflect and ground itself upon the value system shared widely across the society. The services of the good doctor Ramaphosa won't be necessary anymore.

---

155 M. du Preez, "Ramaphosa is courting Malema: Why it could backfire", *News24*, 13 March 2018. Available at: https://www.news24.com/Columnists/Max-duPreez/ramaphosa-is-courting-malema-why-it-could-backfire-20180313 (accessed 23 March 2018).

Fortunately, the conditions on the ground are such that the ANC will probably find it difficult to make it past the 60% threshold. For one thing, instead of focusing mainly on campaigning for the elections, the party will have to defend itself against allegations of state capture. Once the Zondo commission of inquiry into state capture makes its findings, there is no way that the ANC as a political party will not be implicated. Some of the money that has been siphoned from state-owned enterprises such as Eskom and Transnet must have made its way to financing party activities. The truth will find its way out and will definitely implicate the ANC. Voters will as a result hold back on giving the party a strong mandate in 2019.

Ramaphosa has been quite adventurous in the first months of his presidency, making sweeping changes with the intention of getting results as soon as yesterday. He needs to hold back because too many rapid changes expose him unnecessarily to political danger. Unlike Jacob Zuma, who claimed until his last days in office that the people still loved him, Ramaphosa has no proof yet that the people love him, because he has not taken the ANC to an election and won. He should also not try to win overwhelmingly in the 2019 elections, because it is not to his advantage to do so. A moderate win will do just fine for him. Hence Ramaphosa needs to undertake only moderate measures before the elections take place. Whenever he encounters the urge to rock the boat, he should immediately refrain.

Ramaphosa should not get carried away by the euphoria surrounding his presidency. Euphoria can be intoxicating. All presidents in South Africa have had their moments of euphoria, but it is usually short-lived. Therefore, instead of undertaking major policy shifts because he believes everybody loves him, Ramaphosa should seek a mandate for some of the big issues before stamping his authority. Ramaphosa should be careful, for instance, if he decides to restructure the SOEs before 2019. If he wins then, he can implement his project with less resistance from the nation.

In the final instance, the 2019 elections are for the ANC and Ramaphosa to lose. At present, the opposition parties are struggling to inflict damage on his presidency. It was quite telling that when Ramaphosa was nominated as president in Parliament, the opposition could not even name their own alternative candidates, as they have usually done in the past. Ramaphosa was elected unanimously. The EFF remains the only party with an ability to harm Ramaphosa. However, he seems to have a strategy to deal with them, and they seem to have a strategy to extract some concessions from him, as they have already done with expropriation of land without compensation. The other opposition parties, such as the DA, will have to wake up quickly from their slumbers, bestir themselves and gather their thoughts as to how they will deal with Ramaphosa as ANC leader. Still, I do not think the opposition will inflict sufficient damage on Ramaphosa to put the ANC in danger of losing the elections.

Ramaphosa has been waiting for his chance to be president for many years. For a long time it looked as if he would never get the opportunity to lead South Africa. After all these years it is now, at last, Ramaphosa's turn. The question is: will the ANC allow him to truly turn the party and the country around?

Acknowledgements

Writing a book is never an easy task and it is not possible to complete such a project without the support of colleagues, friends and family. Thank you to everyone who supported me in the writing of this book. This includes my publisher, Maryna Lamprecht, who encouraged me to consider contributing another instalment to the story of South Africa's ongoing democratic consolidation. Her patience, guidance and tenacity throughout the process have always made the project look achievable. Thank you to Russell Martin for editing this book and giving clarity to my thoughts and analysis. I would also like to acknowledge every journalist whose probing questions about South African politics have always stimulated me to inquire even further. Their work, by shining a light, helps this nation gain a better understanding of the state of things.

I will always be indebted to my wife, Margaret, for encouraging me to keep on trying to find a better explanation for the events and the world around us. Her support puts it all into perspective.

Index

 RALPH MATHEKGA is a South African author and one of the country's leading political analysts and columnists. His first book, *When Zuma Goes*, was published in 2016. He has taught politics at the University of the Western Cape and worked as a senior policy analyst at the National Treasury. He is often quoted by both local and international media, and he comments regularly on television and radio. Ralph is currently completing a PhD in politics. He is a Senior Researcher working on revolutionary constitutions at the Centre for Humanities Research, University of the Western Cape. He and his wife, Margaret, live in Johannesburg.